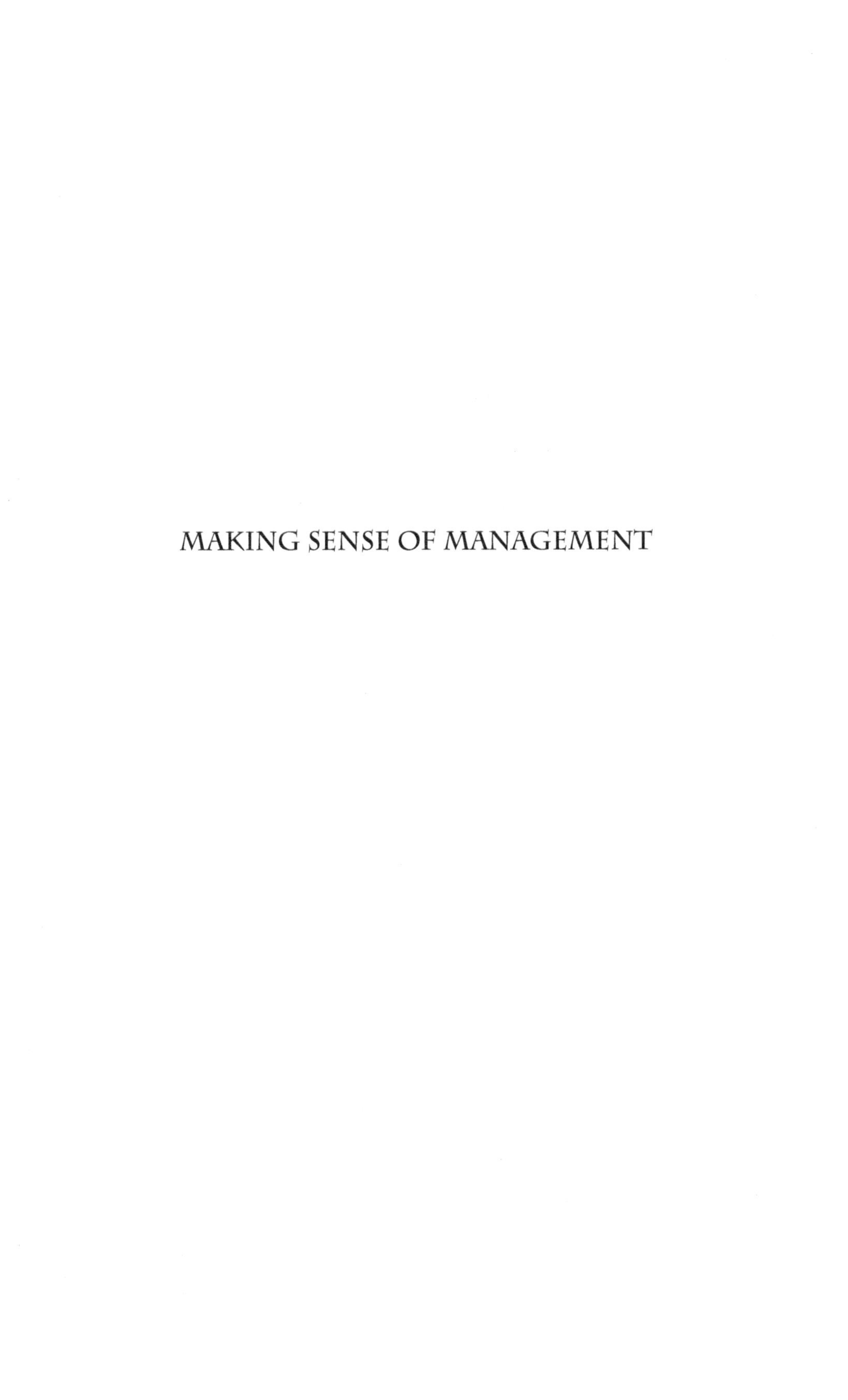

MAKING SENSE OF MANAGEMENT

MAKING SENSE OF MANAGEMENT

A Professional Memoir

JOHN HOWARD STANFORD

An Animal Mitchell Publication
Amenia, New York

Printed in the United States of America

Library of Congress Control Number: 2011932563
ISBN: 9781936940066

Animal Mitchell Publications
POB 260
Amenia, New York 12501

order via:
AnimalMitchell.com

For Betty

Putting It Together

Bit by bit,
Putting it together...
Piece by piece —
Only way to make a work of art.

Every moment makes a contribution,
Every little detail plays a part.
Having just the vision's no solution.
Everything depends on execution:

Putting it together —
That's what counts.

— Lyrics by Stephen Sondheim from
Sunday in the Park With George

CONTENTS

ABOUT THIS BOOK

IT HAS TAKEN about fifty years to write this book – fifty years which I have spent as a student of management, a management analyst, a working manager, and a management teacher. It has taken that long for me to live it and to put it together.

I am still learning. As Le Corbusier, the architect, said of himself, "I live in the skin of a student." I hope I always will.

That is the first message of this book:

The Most Important Thing in Management is to Learn How to Keep On Learning

Management is not simple. No one ever knows it all or can do it all. There is always something more to learn. You don't have to understand everything. But you ought to keep on learning – and unlearning.

Somebody said that the purpose of learning is to proceed "from cocksure ignorance to thoughtful uncertainty." I believe that is true of management. If I had written this book thirty or even twenty years ago, I would have given much more specific answers. Do this. Don't do that. Follow this rule. Learn to do it that way. Now I see many more possibilities and many more uncertainties. The more you learn, the more possibilities you see. The more you understand, the more uncertainties you feel.

The important thing is to keep on learning – from experience (your own and others), from management books (good and bad), from everything that happens in your life (at work and at play).

There is No One Best Way to Manage.

That is a second important message of this book. There are lots of ways to manage. The more of them you know about, the better.

Almost any way of managing can sound plausible. Be a tough boss. Be a sensitive leader. Control everything. Let people alone. Build work groups. Encourage individual initiative. Cooperate. Compete. Be open to change. Avoid fads. Almost any way of managing might actually be good – somewhere, some of the time, for some people, in some situations, for some purposes. In spite of what you may have been told – or sold – no way of managing is always best all the time and for everyone.

Some ways of managing will feel better to you personally. Some will fit better with your particular skills and ideas. Some will work better in a given organization or for what you are trying to do at the time. Any way of managing has to be tailored to fit you and what you are trying to do.

The real trick is to learn ways of managing which you can use and which fit the situation at hand. You need a variety of ways to manage and a wise sense of when and how to apply them – all things considered. It is not a matter of following a recipe. There is no instruction manual.

It is more like "If this is the situation and you want to get this and this and this and this done and not cause that and that and that and that, here are some of the ways you might try to do it and here are some of the results you might expect; now, go ahead and figure out the rest of it for yourself and keep on trying until you learn to get it right (or right enough)."

This book will show you examples of that process. You may be surprised, but that is the way it works, at least in my experience. There are possibilities and there are limits. There are no guarantees and no simple answers. Beware of those who offer them.

Management is a Performing Art

Management may seem remote, abstract, quantitative and impersonal – a matter of power and structure and process and mission and strategy and "bottom lines" rather than of real human beings and human feelings. Some people are put off by this and want to have as little to do with management as possible. Others are attracted by the idea and want to become master technicians who manipulate the controls of organizational machines. I believe both are wrong, misled by a wrong image.

Management in my experience is better understood in terms of a quite different metaphor. Management is an art – primarily a performing art. Managers play roles, the roles they are assigned and the roles they choose. Managers constantly interact with other people — sometimes improvising spontaneously and sometimes acting out very carefully prepared scripts.

Although part of the role of managers is to provide symbolic images for the organization, they remain (up close, at least) quite human. Although they often act with exceptional skill, many are quite unable to explain in words just what it is they do or how they do it. Like most performing arts, management is not easily encapsulated in words. It is best observed in action.

We can observe ourselves and we can observe others in action, performing. We can plan what we intend to do and we can assess afterward what happened. We can learn from our experiences and from the experiences of others. We can think and practice and rehearse and assess and evaluate and all those other things we do as managers to get a sense of what is happening. Ultimately, however, managing is in that moment of acting, of performing, of doing something — and in the responses of others and our responses to them.

When a good jazz group gets it all together, the musical patterns are predictable but each particular performance is unique. It happens spontaneously in the moment and will not happen again in quite the same way. Many of the patterns of management are predictable too, and each performance is unique.

We need to think about management more in terms of art and performance and interactions and not just in terms of science and analysis and control. Over the years, I have come to believe that what managers do (or could do) is more complex than we really understand — probably more complex than we ever will understand

Awareness of management research and theories and techniques is useful. It helps us see patterns and understand relationships and predict effects. It challenges us with unexpected and contradictory insights. It cannot tell us fully how to manage or what goals and values should prevail. Somehow we have to figure out for ourselves what to do and how to do it

That is where the art lies — in putting it all together appropriately and effectively, in real organizations, with real people, in real (and always somewhat unique) situations. Merely applying theory or technique is never enough. Merely imitating the behavior of managers we have worked for and observed is not enough either. Worse is to constantly say one thing and do another, as some managers do, or to reduce the role to fit their own limited range.

The art of management, fully performed, demands high levels of awareness and creativity and self-expression and communication. It transcends its literal elements – people in offices, talking, listening, reading, interacting, walking around, coming and going – and has at its heart a mystery, never fully understood: how do organizations really work? At their best, organizations in action are more than the sum of their parts, and people working together are capable of more than anyone expects.

This book is about one manager's lifelong quest, seeking to experience and to understand the art of management. Telling about some incidents along the way may help you as you undertake your own quest – as a manager, as a potential manager, or simply as one who lives and works in a world of organizations and managers.

Which beings me to another major message:

Everybody Ought to Be a Manager (To Some Extent).

Not everyone could or should become a manager in the sense of filling an executive position in a large organization. However, we would be much better off if more people of intelligence, humanity, sensitivity and humor were drawn to management positions and if those who find themselves unexpectedly in management positions did not tend to act out the worst stereotypes of the role while letting their best abilities atrophy.

Whether or not we ever fill a management position, however, most of us live our work lives in organizations. All of us are heavily influenced by organizations. For all of us, some understanding of how organizations work and of what managers do and how they do it can be a survival skill. You may not want to be a manager, but you should understand enough to cope with a world of organizations and managers

Actually, everyone in an organization has opportunities to manage. Managing is not something you suddenly start to do when you finally reach a certain rung on the ladder. Getting things done in organizations (which is what managers specialize in) is something everyone does to some extent. All of us can learn to do it better.

In the name of "good management" some supervisors and managers try to monopolize the decision-making. Don't be misled by this. Management is too important to be left to a small group of managers in an organization.

You can at least practice some self-management. Nobody else will do that for you, and nobody can entirely prevent you from doing it. You have at least a few choices on the job. Use them. You work with at least a few other people. Learn to work with them better.

Start thinking of yourself as managing (to some extent). Instead of just wondering why "they" don't run things better or assuming "they" must know what they are doing, think about the things you can do something about and do something about them.

This book may help you see how to apply management thinking now, not later. It is likely to make work more interesting and satisfying. It may even change the way you think about yourself and your work

Which leads to the final introductory message:

Managing Can Be Enjoyable.

Do not take too seriously the traditional cries of anguish and pain from some managers, those familiar pleas for us to sympathize with their unhappy lot. All jobs, including management jobs, have their downside, their bad days, their frustrations. The truth is that a good match of manager and role and organization provides a more enjoyable situation than many managers like to admit. We are more likely to hear of executive stress and overload and burnout and of the lonely burdens of life at the top, especially when pay and benefits are in question.

The fact is that managing is often rewarding and sometimes a joy – if, of course you like that sort of thing. If it becomes unbearable (and certainly that can happen), managers should be better situated than most other employees to do something about it.

So whether you are already a manager or would like to be one or hate the idea of managing or are uncertain but curious – this book is for you.

Some Further Explanations

I talk a lot about my own experiences in this book, but not because they are in themselves important or exceptional. They are not. They are ordinary experiences of an ordinary manager in ordinary organizations. I use them because they are real and because they are what I know best. They show how ideas about management can be expressed in daily work life and how such ideas change and develop through work experiences.

I know that what I recall is not the complete story. Memories fade and recollections are inaccurate. I saw things, as all managers do, from my own point of view. Others would undoubtedly recall differently, if at all. I have tried to be truthful, accurate, and fair. I have changed some names and omitted others to protect privacy. I apologize for any errors or misrepresentations. What you read is what I remember – no more and no less.

You will find me expressing my personal opinions – what I think I learned about management from these experiences. These are presented as personal, not universal, truths. Respond to them as you will. You may see different lessons to be learned, different meanings. Fair enough. True or false, right or wrong, these notes illustrate a learning process which you may apply in your own way for your own purposes.

I simply hope that it will affect the way you think about managers and organizations and the way you relate to them

John H Stanford

PART ONE

BECOMING A MANAGER

Snapshot (1946)

WHEN *I THINK OF MYSELF* at twenty-seven, I picture a very young man arriving a few months after the end of World War II at the scorchingly hot, elm-tree shaded, flat, Central Valley town of Sacramento – a provincial River City, the capitol of California. I think of my newly-bought pre-war green Plymouth coupe and of my few possessions (clothes, books, records and record player) stashed in the trunk of the car. I think of the Victorian boarding house across the street from Capitol Park where four of us shared a third-floor room.

At that time I was feeling hopeful but uncertain: after seventeen years of school and three restless war years in the Air Forces, I felt ready to settle somewhere. But...here? Was this the long-awaited beautiful post-war world? Well, actually, for me, maybe yes.

My picture of myself at the time was I think fairly realistic: unimpressive looks (short, blond, glasses); emotionally underdeveloped (somewhat of a loner, with no deep attachments); socially agreeable (able to get along in groups, but quietly); mentally somewhat of a whiz kid (a high academic achiever); culturally well developed (avid reader, classical and jazz pianist, jazz record collector, fan of all the performing arts, architecture buff); politically liberal (believer in social action for the common good and in progress through democratic reforms); religiously inactive (a Baptist upbringing had left scars); both an exceptional achiever and somewhat of a wimp.

I saw myself then as rational, organized, capable but unfocused. I had great expectations but didn't know what to expect. I was confident that some day I would do important things, but right then doubted my ability to do any job really well. I felt that youthful blend of confidence and anxiety.

And enthusiasm. Despite its unimpressive Sacramento setting, California's State Government attracted and excited me. Governor Earl Warren, a moderate Republican with progressive ideas, was then in his first term – and increasingly popular with both parties. He was recruiting competent professionals to head departments and achieving a reputation for good government: honesty, integrity and leadership for a rapidly growing state.

By the time I was drafted I had already earned a Masters degree in Public Administration, had worked a few months in Washington, D.C., in the wartime Office for Emergency Management. In the Air Forces I had spent three years as a Personnel Officer in the Air Transport Command. It made sense to see a temporary appointment as a Junior Administrative Analyst in the Finance Department as a real opportunity. It was good for six months, and if I could score well enough on the next open civil service examination it could last longer.

Chapter One

ANALYZING MANAGEMENT

THE BASIC IDEA of Management Analysis was to use applied research methods to help improve administration and solve administrative problems. It was part of a Public Administration movement which tried to combine the values of scientific management, business administration and good government. Scientific management applied engineering to the workplace. Business administration provided university-educated professional managers. The progressive vision of good government was that non-political professionals would apply the principles of administration in an efficient and economical public service.

The movement fit neatly within the larger trend toward a more professional public service in many fields and a non-political merit system of career employment. Even before World War II, some California cities and counties had university-trained professional managers. Now, the State (whose Director of Finance was a former city manager) was moving in this direction, developing small central staffs of specialists in finance, budgeting, accounting, auditing, purchasing, and – now – management analysis.

All of these "new" specialties had in common a desire to strengthen the role of the Governor as chief executive officer and to centralize administrative services. Most State agencies at the time were still operating in an older tradition – a loose confederation of paternalistically operated little fiefdoms. Each had its own legislative and political support, its clientele, and its special interests. The heads of such agencies seldom thought of themselves as managers.

Central budgeting, central purchasing and central personnel administration had already begun to have an impact. As State government began its rapid postwar growth the old ways tended to persist in the long-established agencies, but new units were being added and staffed with new specialists. There was a certain dynamic tension between the comfortable old ways and the impersonal new ways, but with a strong Governor, an urge to create new State programs, and a general confidence in progress and change, the balance of power was with the new.

The latest example of the trend – the Management Analysis Staff – had been established in the Department of Finance only a few months before I arrived. Its mission was to be an in-house management consulting service, making studies of the organization, staffing, and administrative operations of State agencies for the Governor, the Director, or other State officials. It was at the time a group of about six people, headed by a Chief Analyst – a very small unit with a very large potential (depending on how useful it turned out to be).

To give a more close-up view of this kind of work, let me tell you a bit about my first assignment: make an administrative survey of the California Horse Racing Board; analyze its organization, staff requirements, and administrative activities and recommend improvements.

The study had been requested by the chair of the Board, a prominent Los Angeles attorney appointed by the Governor. Since the end of the war, horse racing in California had been increasing rapidly. My impression is that he and the Secretary (the Board-appointed head of the fifteen-person office in Los Angeles) hoped the study would get them a bigger budget and more staff than they had so far been able to get from the Finance department budget analysts.

The initial contacts went well. Everyone seemed friendly and cooperative. I enjoyed visiting the Del Mar track with the Secretary, meeting officials and owners. I enjoyed watching races from the Board box and going backstage to see how parimutuel betting worked. I enjoyed talking to the Secretary about his years as a race track official. What I did not enjoy was that soon I would be expected to tell him how to make the agency work better. I felt like a well-received imposter, likely to be exposed at any moment.

So I asked a lot of questions and listened very carefully. I took careful notes. People interested in their work are often happy to talk about it, even with someone who is a kind of investigator. It is often a novel and flattering experience just to be asked. I also looked at a lot of records and reports.

Each evening I went over my notes and thought about what I needed to know next. The more we talked, the better acquainted we were. The better acquainted, the freer the discussion became. The freer the discussion, the more I learned.

Among other things, I learned that the employees in this little independent agency (mostly field investigators and clerks) knew a lot about horse racing but not much about State administration. They were genuinely worried about the growing workload, but unsure what to do about it. They did not expect me to know much about horse racing (right!), but assumed (since I had been sent from Sacramento by the Director of Finance) that I knew all about State administration (wrong!).

So the next aspect of the study was to make careful notes of things involving State budgeting or accounting or personnel or purchasing or other central administrative systems. I planned to follow up on these later, back in Sacramento. Meanwhile, I could say, without embarrassment, "I don't know, but I will find out," and move on to the next topic.

Knowing how much central staff people like and need numbers, I used the records to compile figures on workload and staffing and backlogs – statistics which had not been available in Sacramento. Staff analysts get tired of being asked for more of everything simply because the agency "needs" it. They stop really hearing unless they see some data – particularly some numbers which they can feel are objective and reasonably reliable. I felt I would be trusted and helped somewhat by my staff colleagues in Sacramento, but that I would be more likely to get acceptance of proposals if people could say, "OK. I didn't have that information before," instead of "Oh. You are saying that I was wrong?"

The data was there. It was just a matter of having the time and interest and of understanding the need. To the Board staff, much more interested in horse racing than in budgets, it had seemed enough to say what they needed. To The Budget staff, much more interested in accounting and financial analysis than in horse racing, words were merely opinions but numbers were facts. They wanted facts, especially when the activity was unfamiliar and distant. I sympathized with both and undertook to bridge the gap.

The other essential for this kind of analytical work was to organize the paper. As I rapidly accumulated material and ideas, I worried that I might lose control of the mounting stacks of paper and wind up with a confused mess instead of a completed survey. Fortunately, I had learned as a graduate student doing academic research the kind of careful planning and recording an analyst needs. Keep track of what you have done and need to do. Record information accurately and systematically. Organize material logically, cross-check and verify. Keep track of sources. Review raw notes promptly and make sure they are complete and usable. In short, leave as complete a paper trail as possible of your process and your information.

This was not mere paper shuffling. For example, by organizing and cross-checking I discovered that although the Board was asking for more staff and a larger budget it already had four positions approved and funded in earlier budgets which were not being used. They were vacant because they were not the kind of positions needed now. Once discovered, it reduced the net increase needed from six positions to two.

Not everything in a survey can be resolved so simply and so objectively. I worried about my ability to make valid judgments about larger issues. For example, the Board wanted to hire and pay directly the stewards and other track officials instead of merely licensing them. I felt uncomfortable basing a recommendation on my personal opinion, uncomfortable in trying to apply some vague principle of administration, and even more uncomfortable about not dealing with the issue at all.

The solution in this case was one which is often appropriate in surveys of government agencies: check it against the laws. Everything a State agency does has to be based on some law which authorizes it (unlike private businesses, which in general can do something unless some law prohibits it).

In this case, I found that the horse racing laws authorized the Board to regulate the tracks, not to operate them. It was supposed to see that the tracks carried out their responsibilities, not to take over responsibilities. However, the law already gave the Board more authority over track officials than it was using. If it wanted to do more than merely license them it could decide to appoint and remove them directly. On the other hand, if track officials were to be paid directly by the Board the law required that they be employed under civil service procedures, which would be extremely difficult (or the State constitution would have to be amended by the voters to exempt them from civil service). In short, review of applicable laws (with the help of staff lawyers) went a long way toward suggesting a practical response to this policy proposal: use the authority you already have to do what you want to do in a simpler and easier way.

Only one other area of the survey needs to be mentioned: the review of organization. Most administrative surveys at the time involved some review of organization. There was a great deal of confidence at that time in what were called principles of good organization. Organizations were assumed to operate better if organized according to these principles and worse if they were not. A lot of work went into studies to "streamline" the organization structure, to "modernize" it, to (as one colleague used to say) "eliminate the outhouses on the organization chart."

It seemed to me that this was quite a different kind of analysis. One did not get the facts, analyze them, and develop solutions. One started with the principles, checked whether the organization fit them, and (if not) recommended the principles be applied. It was not difficult work. You mostly checked (or prepared) organization charts, reviewed (or wrote) job descriptions, checked the lines of command and applied the check-list of principles. It was not necessary to pay much attention to how well or poorly the organization worked; that was somewhat irrelevant. The other assumption (usually unstated) was that improving organization structure would always be worth the effort and the cost of changing.

What sort of rules did the principles provide? Here are a few specifications for design of a "good" organization:

1. Does each position report clearly to one and only one superior? It should.

2. Is the agency headed by a single executive (rather than a group)? It should be.

3. If there is a board, is it doing administrative work? It should not be.

4. Does the agency report clearly to the chief executive (in this case, the Governor)? It should.

5. Do too many or too few people report to one person? They shouldn't.

6. Are there too many or too few levels in the organization? There shouldn't be.

7. Is there a current organization chart? There should be.

8. Are there current duties statements for each position in the organization? There should be.

9. So it goes... (I am not making this up – only simplifying a little.)

The Horse Racing Board was a very small organization which seemed to me to work informally and well. I proposed to just omit any mention of structure, since I had no change to propose. At this point I discovered some other rules of management analysis (at least as practiced in that staff at that time): (1) For every study there has to be a written report; (2) The report has to follow a standard report format and use impersonal language (for example, every recommendation has to begin "It is recommended that..."); (3) There has to be a finding for every item contained in the survey assignment. It was very logical (I thought) and very rigid (I felt).

Anyway, I ran down the checklist and dreamed up a recommendation about organization: as the staff increased, the Board should delegate more administrative authority to the Secretary (based on the principle that boards should not do administrative work). There was now a recommendation on organization. The study was now complete.

What happened after the report was issued? As I recall, the recommendations about staffing and budget were implemented. The other administrative recommendations were generally accepted by the agency and its staff.

What did the survey accomplish? That question could be answered from several points of view:

1. The Board chair got the attention he wanted for his small agency. He received more staff and more funds, although not as much as he had requested.

2. The Board staff also got some of the help they wanted plus some unasked-for advice. They too received attention to their problems.

3. The central Budget staff could feel that they had been right in their initial reluctance to give the agency the increase it wanted. The study gave more information, but left the budget decision in their hands.

4. Similarly, the central Personnel staff could use the report in establishing job classifications and pay levels, but clearly retained control of these decisions.

5. The Finance Director was able to respond positively to the concerns of an important appointee of the Governor without having to say yes or no at the time. It put him in the role of a manager.

6. The Chief Analyst was pleased because the clients were pleased and because the study contributed in a small way toward acceptance of the new analysis staff and its program.

7. I felt I was off to a good start. This was work I enjoyed and for which I felt I had some talent. The idea of becoming a manager was not in my mind, but I was beginning to learn how State government worked and how to get things done.

After the Horse Racing Board Study I spent four years doing such studies in many State agencies. They covered a wide range of programs, people and problems, but some of the elements of that first study remained constant:

- Get the facts and analyze them.

- Draw a line between politics and administration, and concentrate on improving administration.

- Be as objective and fair as possible, but also be sensitive to people and open to their contributions.

- Take time to do thorough and reliable work.

- Leave a clear trail of your work and document the sources on which your report is based.

- Make a full report of your findings, recommendations and reasons.

In time I was able to go through the process much faster, take fewer wrong turns, consider a wider range of factors and solutions, be more persuasive. I was accumulating more skills as an analyst and more understanding of State government. My most valuable asset, however, was the fact that I was allowed to take enough time on each assignment to do the best work of which I was capable. Although my draft reports were reviewed and edited carefully, I was never told what to recommend or not to recommend; that responsibility was clearly mine, and I took it very seriously. If my work was questioned (as it sometimes was), it was up to me to explain and justify and take primary responsibility for it.

One other tool of the analyst trade is worth a special mention. It was perhaps my secret weapon: the help of a good library and a professional librarian. There is a danger that if each study is approached as if it were new and unique one may overlook useful information from the past and from studies of similar problems in other governments. At that time, the State Library in Sacramento had an extensive collection of government documents and publications. It was poorly indexed, but fortunately was in the charge of a wonderful librarian who had a detailed personal knowledge of the collection, an ability to locate non-obvious but useful sources, and an unlimited enthusiasm for being helpful. She also had access to the University of California research libraries.

A word to her about a survey assignment would soon result in a table-top full of well-chosen reports, legislation, hearing reports and other publications relating to the subject. I never ceased to be amazed at how few people seemed aware of this great information service. Today, with all the technology available for information search and retrieval, that kind of personal and professional service is still in my mind the ideal.

I also learned that it was absolutely necessary to work closely and cooperatively with people in the agency under study. This way of working seemed an obvious advantage for all concerned, but unfortunately it was not always the practice. It could be much more comfortable for an analyst to remain aloof, avoiding the give-and-take of informal contact in the name of objectivity and independence. It could be much easier to use the initial anxiety or protective reaction of agency people as a justification for remaining at a distance. It could be tempting to stay safely back in one's own office rather than setting up camp within the agency during a study (and having less contact with peers and supervisors for extended periods). But in my experience the more initiative an analyst takes during a study to establish and maintain communication, the greater the likelihood that the study results will be successful.

Besides learning to do administrative surveys, the work involved a lot of incidental learning which in the long run was just as valuable. (This is true, I believe, in most jobs: there are many less obvious opportunities for learning if you look for them). For example:

- The physical setting. We were located in the capitol building, the symbolic and literal center of State government. Nearby were the public galleries of the legislative chambers and the committee hearing rooms. We could drop in for a first-hand view of important debates and hearings. The Governor and his staff were nearby; I remember the time Governor Warren had us all in for punch and Christmas carols (I played the piano). The elevator operator always had the latest stock quotes (he was rumored to be wealthy). We shared a large room with most of the Budget staff, and unavoidably had a ringside seat for some of their more heated debates with agency people. If you needed to know something about State government, there were plenty of people in the building to ask. It was like living in a company town.

- The Management Analysis staff was a small and close-knit group within this capitol community. We shared a lot of common background and professional interests. We lunched together. We shop-talked together. We helped each other. We learned from each other. We even folk-danced together (the Chief Analyst loved to folk dance). We believed in what we were doing and we wanted it to succeed. (At the time, I rather took that for granted; now I see how important it was.)

- As we moved through State government on our assignments, we built a network of associates with whom we were in touch and to whom we could turn for help. One of the great limitations of many working-level jobs is that you are limited to relatively few inside contacts - limited by time, by rank, by protocol, by location, by habit. Bureaucracies put people in boxes. Top executives have the over-all view, but may lack knowledge of the supporting details and the rank-and-file staff. We administrative analysts, on the other hand, were travelers, always on the move, always learning more about the territory, always making new contacts and renewing old ones. One reason staff people can become so useful in large organizations is that being free to move around they can develop a practical sense both of the grass-roots operations and the over-all organization. Like middle managers, they can he fill a gap between the two.

- Professional organizations. Another meeting place for like-minded staff people from various organizations was at local chapters of professional societies. One could get a different view, learn from fellow members, promote the profession, and practice organizational and social skills.

- Sacramento, the city. At the time, State government was (aside from buying and selling real estate) the biggest game in town. Its impact was everywhere. You couldn't help being aware of it. Your neighbors probably worked there. Your newspapers focused on it. Your friendships centered there. It may have been insular, but for those on the inside it was the center of the world.

I learned a lot about management from being a management analyst, and I learned a lot about management from being in the center of State government, and I learned a lot about management from being in Sacramento. After four years of this, I became more aware of what I was not learning: I was spending my time telling people how to improve operations, but I had not had the experience of practicing what I was preaching. It gradually became clear that I would probably become a perennial administrative analyst unless I got some actual administrative experience, and for that I was prepared to leave Sacramento, if necessary. I was still not thinking about becoming a manager, but I wanted a wider range of career options. (It can be very important in a career to understand what you are not learning and when to invest in a job change; you only get a limited number of chances.)

Chapter Two

SERVING MANAGEMENT

I *WAS BEGINNING* to feel a need for hands-on experience in some State agency. At about this time the State Personnel Board established a new series of job classifications called Administrative Service Officer. The idea was that administrative support services in State agencies involved the same activities (personnel, budget, accounting, purchasing, facilities, etc.) regardless of the kind of programs the agency operated. The series provided four grade levels, I to IV, based on the size and complexity of the organization.

It was a new concept in State government, and one not widely accepted in the operating departments. Until then, each agency had usually thought of itself as having unique requirements, and wanted to appoint someone to handle its administrative affairs who was already familiar with its programs. Often this meant appointing someone already in the agency.

The central personnel staff believed that a career ladder of administrative service positions would attract people with more general administrative skills to State service and that ultimately the work would be done better by such specialists. It was another aspect of the post-war trend in California State government to recognize administration and management as a distinct professional field. To the central agency staffs, the prospect of having more people in State departments like themselves seemed like progress. To some of the agencies it was merely one more example of what they saw as increasing interference by the new central bureaucrats.

The State Personnel Board staff launched the new concept with a series of open competitive exams, hoping to attract new people for the new classifications. With the help of my military experience, I qualified for the lowest level, Grade I, and came out high enough on the list to be referred for interview when the first vacancy occurred – in the Department of Insurance in San Francisco.

When the department and I first met, it was not love at first sight. I learned later that the Insurance department had opposed using the new classification, but had reluctantly yielded to the central personnel staff's insistence.

The department's first choice had been one of its employees who had filled the job on a temporary basis but had not done well enough on the examination to be appointed permanently. The initial interview went fairly well, but I sensed that they were skeptical of my qualifications – obviously I knew nothing about insurance – and would have preferred to appoint someone who did.

For my part, I could see the advantage of getting this type of experience, but it meant moving at my own expense from Sacramento to San Francisco with a very small increase in pay. The Chief Analyst advised me to stay where I was. He pointed out (as several people did) that I would be moving away from the center of State government to a small, specialized agency which was not even in the capitol city. Others told me that the Insurance department (although it ranked high among state insurance agencies at the time) was not very up-to-date in its management and that I might not be able to have much impact there. It might turn out to be a limited and limiting dead-end job.

On the other hand, there were few other State jobs for which I was eligible. If I wanted to return later to administrative analysis work, I would be better qualified. Experience at the first level of the new administrative service officer series would open additional possibilities for advancement. Although the Insurance department was small (about 200 people, at the time) it was a separate agency which had on a small scale all the elements of larger departments, so the experience would be useful in any other department.

I decided that the best strategy for me would be to go from the center of State government (where I merely gave administrative advice) to the grass-roots of a State agency (where I would be in charge of administrative services). I thought of it as a kind of extended special assignment or project which would last at least two or three years but not indefinitely. (I was still not thinking in terms of becoming a manager, but clearly I was hoping by this time for a public service career in administrative work.)

All things considered, the Department offered me the job. All things considered, I accepted it. We both hoped our decisions would turn out well.

What was it like, handling administrative services for the Insurance department? What are "administrative services," anyway? How do they support the management of an agency? What can you learn in such an assignment?

For me, the difference in location was drastic: I went from the working in the center of the Capitol area, where State buildings and State employees were dominant, to modest upper-floor offices in an old theater building on upper Market Street near the Civic center.

The Insurance department had traditionally occupied rather upscale space in the downtown financial district, near the offices of large insurance companies. The Finance department had recently forced the department to move to this less expensive space which Finance officials had rented as part of a master lease with a major owner of office space. The Insurance Commissioner was angry at being forced to move to less desirable offices. For several months he had refused to approve paying the rent, until he found out that the Finance department was making the payments anyway. For me it was enough to get to work anywhere in glamorous downtown San Francisco and to live in the exciting Bay Area instead of in provincial Sacramento.

The biggest difference from administrative analysis was the faster pace and wider variety of day-by-day work. An analyst works slowly and carefully on a few projects at a time. The most important thing is to do a thorough and complete job of applied research. Theoretically, an administrative service officer presides over a set of smooth-running, efficient and reliable services which run so well that people in the department can take them for granted. Actually, a lot of my days turned out to be barely controlled chaos.

It was my wife who first observed that my Friday afternoons seemed to be particular crisis times; I found Monday mornings also to be difficult – perhaps some people tended to become emotional just before the end of a workweek or just before the start of a new one or, it often seemed, both.

There were so many people who could make work for you: people in the department, people in the central staff agencies, people in the industry, people in the legislative offices, people wanting to sell you something, people with complaints, people needing something, people making demands, people making judgments. It seemed as if every phone call, every mail delivery, every conversation would bring a new piece of work of some kind – and there were not very many opportunities to pass it along to someone else. The name of the game seemed to be just do it – and mostly do it yourself.

I soon learned that work did not come with neat little labels – "personnel policy," "budget request," "public relations problem" – nor was it always apparent whether it was a simple routine matter or a complex potential crisis.

As an administrative service officer, your days are filled with small events. Somebody needs to hire a replacement. The addressing machine isn't working right. The people in one of the offices are having a quiet battle over whether the windows should be open or closed. The purchasing office is insisting on buying a typewriter brand which some of the secretaries don't like. A division head had decided whom to promote and wants you to put through the paperwork to make it legitimate. The secretary to a top official complains that too many minority people are being hired. The switchboard operator picks up a rumor that other State offices are going to give employees extra informal time off before the next holiday. A member of your staff resigns and wants to leave next week. Three reports are on your desk for review. A long-time employee explodes at you with pent-up anger and frustration, but leaves feeling better because the problems are now yours, too. A personnel analyst from Sacramento needs an hour to go over a draft of the description and qualifications for a new job classification the department will be using. The Commissioner asks for a five-minute staff meeting report tomorrow, covering all the important developments in your area. A friend from another agency calls to suggest lunch and hints of important new developments in Sacramento. A division head brings a proposal for reorganizing the office and wants your reaction right away. In your in-basket are three new administrative regulations from Sacramento, notices of four meetings you ought to attend, copies of two new legislative bills which would affect the department, five letters to sign, ten ads for office supplies and equipment, three requests, two complaints, and one thank-you. Your bus leaves in twenty minutes. So it goes, and goes, and goes. It is like being the housekeeper for a work household of 200 people.

In broad theory, all administrative services involve some unified kind of activity which supports the department's operations. In practice, it is harder to find the common elements. It is easy to be overwhelmed by the details, to lose track of your basic goals, the things you intended to accomplish when you took the job. Besides all that, there is something about a job like this which the textbooks don't tell you: an administrative services officer is also a kind of miscellaneous activities officer. If a job was not part of anyone else's duties, it must be an administrative service function. If it wasn't someone else's problem, it was probably mine.

I don't mean to imply that I did everything myself. There were people to fill out the forms, handle the mail, post the accounts, prepare the payroll, operate the telephone switchboard (yes, there was still at that time a real live operator), keep the personnel records, requisition the supplies, run the lists of insurance licensees, etc. For each of these, there was someone (about a dozen people in all) who knew what to do and how to do it far better than I did. They did the job the way they had learned to do it from somebody else, not me. They took pride in knowing who to call, what forms to use, what rule to apply, where to look it up, what to do. They did not need a newcomer to tell them these things; they did not feel a need for things to change. If something came along which did not fit within their routines, they were happy to pass it along to me. Otherwise, they preferred to be let alone to do their work.

They were good people. Mostly, they wanted to do a good job (as they understood it), to help others (if the rules allowed it), to have work friends (who could help them), to be treated fairly (as they saw it), to be defended (if they followed the rules), to find satisfaction in life at work (in return for a reasonable level of effort) and to have good bosses (who would look out for them personally).

They were also generally respectful of rank and status and authority (if allowed their own self-respect). They accepted orders and changes in the rules obediently (if from a legitimate source). If, however, they were skeptical or opposed to change, they could be frustratingly slow and carefully minimal in their responses. Honest in answering questions, they did not always feel impelled to volunteer what was not specifically asked. In general they had little sense of the broader government or public service environment which was to me so interesting.

These attitudes were not only common among the staff in my office group, they were fairly typical of all the people in the department. They could be tremendously helpful to me, or they could make my work tremendously difficult – depending on what sort of relationships developed between us.

It seemed to me that I had three basic things to do: (1) establish a more favorable opinion in Sacramento of the department's administrative competence, building on my previous experience and contacts there; (2) develop confidence among people in the department in my ability to improve services and to get needed resources from Sacramento; (3) learn more about administrative services while helping others develop and use their talents more fully.

I saw these, however, not as separate goals but as an integral part of each and every contact, every decision, every action – unifying factors which helped make sense of all those day-by-day details. It seemed to me that to make sense of the broad goals, you needed the details, and to make sense of the details, you needed the broad goals, and to make things happen you needed relationships of mutual confidence and trust. (In work of this kind you are never just doing one thing, you are working on several things at the same time, hoping that each step will move things along a bit toward several objectives, large and small. At the same time, you have to keep open and keep improvising because you are never really in control – you are just one part of the situation and it keeps changing. When it all comes together and it works, it feels great! Those are the moments that keep you going, keep you trying, keep you happy. The rest, you tend to forget.)

How to illustrate more specifically this curious interaction between the daily happenings at work and the longer range goals? I need to turn to a particular service activity and follow its development over time as an example of the process: preparing the budget for the department. Bear in mind that similar strategies and tactics had to be shaped for the whole range of administrative services. This is merely one example.

The budget process is a particularly useful example because it is so crucial for an agency. It happens in small steps and small details over a period of several years, but the process taken as a whole is often taken as a kind of index of administrative success. From it comes the money on which operations depend. With more money, more things are possible. With less money, some things become impossible. The dollars reflect the strengths and weaknesses of an agency, its progress and its politics. It is the "bottom" line of public administration.

Within a few months of my arrival, it was time to start preparing the next annual budget. The first step was a quiet informal review of how the department had been handling its budget until now. I studied the documents – the budget laws, procedures, reports, correspondence, the past budgets (the budget process is among other things an accumulation of paperwork details). I asked a lot of questions of my staff, my predecessor, the department managers, the central budget analysts in Sacramento. (If anything, I exaggerated my ignorance in order to encourage people to explain things to me; I didn't have to exaggerate much because I really didn't know much.) I did a lot of listening. Most people enjoy explaining their work or expressing their opinions to a sympathetic and interested listener. This step also allowed initial friendly contacts which would be useful later.

I concluded that the department's handling of the budget had been typical for the time, a traditional playing of the budget game with about the usual results (some wins, some losses, some mutual resentments between the central budget analysts and the agency). Here is how the traditional game is played, with its mix of rhetoric and reality, paper and power:

1. The Governor announces (signs a memo prepared by the central budget agency) that the next fiscal year will be unusually tight and that belt-tightening will be required of

everyone. Reality: pious rhetoric for the record; file and forget.

2. The agency adds up its current expenditures. Any money in the current budget not needed should be subtracted. Reality: Be sure to show that every dollar in the current budget will be spent. Protect that budget base. The agency worked hard to get the money. It would be foolish to give it back. It would make it harder to get money next year.

3. The agency reviews its programs and prepares a minimum budget (with factual justifications) to carry out is legal responsibilities next year. Reality: Carry over the full amount from the current budget. Add an allowance for cost increases. Add money anywhere work is expected to increase; if work is expected to decrease, forget it. Ask agency officials what they would like to have next year. Add them all up. If they total about five to ten percent above current budget base, OK. If not, drop out the more ridiculous ones (or the ones from people least likely to object effectively) to bring the total to about that amount. (To receive requests for less than about 10% increase is extremely unlikely. People understand the game and know the unwritten rule: if you don't ask for more, you may get less. Whatever is requested now will be reduced later in the process, so put money in now to allow for these cuts.)

4. The agency head reviews the budget request and decides on a minimum budget request. Everyone in the agency supports this request during the remaining steps. Reality: The agency head usually looks only at a few major budget issues and leaves most of the details to the budget people. Some will support this budget and some won't, but those in the agency who try to get more than this for themselves should be careful not to be caught. From here on, the agency budget is left primarily to the agency budget staff, who shepherd it through the rest of the process and are supposed to get it approved with as few changes as possible, regardless.

5. The central budget agency and the Governor review the budget requests, hold hearings with agencies on the major issues, and prepare the Governor's budget request to the Legislature. Reality: The process is the same as went on within each agency, but with more players and many more issues. In practice, the central budget agency has more power because few people understand the whole process or the whole budget document, which is comprehensive, technical and complex. The Governor and the top officials can deal personally with only a few issues. The document is put together in a great rush just before the deadline. It is often unclear who made what decisions and why. (This softens the sharp edges of conflict and somewhat obscures the fact that while in theory budget analysts only provide information and advice, in practice they make many important decisions.

6. From here on, everybody on the administrative side (including the State agencies) is supposed to support the Governor's budget. Again, some do and some don't. Those who don't are very careful, very powerful, or (perhaps) very unwise.

7. Financial committees in the Assembly and the Senate of the Legislature, with advice from the Legislature's budget staff, hold hearings on the most significant issues, obtain testimony from the Governor's budget staff and the agencies, and recommend a Budget Bill to the whole Legislature. Differences between the two versions are resolved. Before the new fiscal year begins, a Budget Bill is passed in both houses and signed by the Governor (who may reduce individual appropriation items but not increase them.) Reality: In general the process is a repetition of previous steps, but with additional players and higher stakes. By this time attention focuses mostly on a few items: issues raised by legislative staff, significant political issues, issues raised by some legislators and pressure groups. The central budget staffs keep on working out the details with one another, largely off-stage, while a few big issues take center stage for dramatic

public controversy. Most of the budget is really settled, but agencies continue their watchful waiting in case of an unexpected development. Somehow, sooner or later (usually later) a Budget Bill is passed and signed by the Governor.

8. The central finance agency releases appropriated money to the departments. It has power to control the rate of spending each quarter, to hold back money not needed, to make adjustments during the year, to approve some kinds of expenditures, and generally to monitor financial performance during the budget year. Reality: Most money is allocated and spent routinely without much further central budget attention. Again, a few issues get most of the top-level attention and the rest is left mostly to budget analysts and accountants. During a fiscal year, success for the central budget staff is to "find" money for things somebody important enough wants to do, and to be unable to finance anything else.

9. Soon the primary focus shifts to preparing the budget for the next fiscal year. Several budgets are always in process at the same time: cleaning up after last year's; spending this year's; preparing next year's. This gives those who understand the process the possibility of some juggling among the several concurrent budgets.

10. Auditors check to see if the money was spent properly and managed well. Reality: This happens so separately that it may seem unrelated to what has gone before. The auditors will focus mainly on legality, appropriate fiscal procedures and controls, and accepted accounting practices, although they also like to be regarded as concerned with good management. There will be several audits by several different agencies. They usually agree, but not always.

There is rather little attention to results anywhere along the line. People concerned with the budget process keep most of their attention focused on the future and the present, not the past. Once the money is spent, most people would rather forget it. Budget systems are long on forecasts and expenditure controls and short on reviews of performance and results.

Incidentally, this discussion applies primarily to the operating part of the budget – the money for current expenses. The money for construction and other capital spending has a much longer cycle which may extend over five, ten or even twenty years of planning, budgeting and spending. There is a separate part of the budget for capital outlay. Funds for construction may extend over more than one budget. The whole process is even more specialized and complex than the operating budget. Similar games are played but by different players. (The Insurance department had little capital spending, so I did not learn these games until years later.)

With this background of the budget process – both the rhetoric and the reality – let's get back to the Insurance department budget process as I found it.

The agency budget had been carrying a "float" for several years – positions which had been provided in the budget, but were not actually needed and remained unfilled from year to year. They had been protected as part of the budget base by always estimating they would be filled in the current year and carrying funds for them over into the next budget request. The practice had two advantages for the department. It gave a cushion of jobs and money which could be used, if needed, without having to ask for a budget increase. It made the budget base larger, so that the percentage increase for the next year would be a smaller number. The disadvantage was that the budget was separated from the real situation and that it was less credible to central budget analysts. The central staff sensed what was going on, but had not pinned down the details.

Another traditional aspect of the agency budget was the lack of factual support for requested increases. Whatever managers said they needed was included, along with whatever explanation they had provided, however skimpy. There were few workload numbers and little real information about major programs or needs. It was easy to prepare, but easy to cut when it got to the central budget staff. The agency could blame the central staff for being arbitrary and the budget analysts could feel they were being effective.

The result of such budget practices in the agency had been mediocre – neither very good nor very bad. Continuing and stable programs were quite well funded, and had the added comfort of the budgetary "float." New and changing programs fared less well, and might be pinched or favored, depending on the luck of the budget process. It was a sort of one-size-fits-all system, in which some real needs were unfunded while others were over-budgeted.

For the agency the budget process was a burden, not a tool. They rather grudgingly did the minimum required by the system. For the central agencies, the budget requests were not an adequate basis for review, so they made judgments based on a sense of the agency's administrative competence. Neither had spent much time on the budget process.

There was good reason to expect that this traditional, low-risk, low-gain budgeting would be less satisfactory in the future. The central Finance department was clearly committed to increasingly "professional" budgeting, meaning more demands on agencies for better information. Increasing in size and power, the Finance department could reward or punish agencies according to its sense of their competence and cooperation in administrative matters. The Insurance department could keep on with its old budgetary ways, but would eventually be forced to meet the new demands.

The Insurance department itself was heading into a much less stable environment. Issues of rate regulation and consumer protection and licensing standards meant more changes in its programs. The possibility of Federal entrance into insurance regulation was causing some to want more active State insurance agencies. The department would need to develop more trust in its administrative competence in order to get more recognition of its new budgetary needs.

What I looked for was a "win-win" budget strategy, an approach which would fit the situation, improve results, benefit all concerned (including me) and not hurt anybody. What emerged in my thinking as the most feasible and the most likely to succeed was also the most simple and straightforward: I undertook to build a better budget. Forget the game-playing, I decided. Make the budget according to the rules, not the usual reality. Make it honest. Make it minimum. Make it complete. Make it the best budget I can make. Hope that the others involved – in the agency and in the central budget office – will respond positively to the change and to me.

So I did the unthinkable: I built a budget which voluntarily cut back money and positions in the current budget – cut them back below what had already been approved, "gave back" the money. I also developed massive amounts of what budget analysts love best: workload figures. For each major program of the department, I picked something countable and counted it (number of insurers, licensees, investigations, rate reviews, receiverships, etc. I dug up workload figures for the past five years and used them as a basis for projected changes.

Instead of asking for everything anyone thought of, only the most clearly needed additions went into the budget request. Each was supported by workload information and by careful job descriptions and justification statements. All of the required accounting and budgeting tables were checked and rechecked to make sure they complied fully with the current budget instructions and were error-free.

In total, the budget request for the next year was about the same as the amount already approved for the current year. The requested increases were less than the voluntary decreases in the current year. We were saying, in effect, in the logic of budgeting, workload is increasing, but we can get along with an appropriation about the same as last time.

What happened? Without over-all increase, the budget was relatively non-controversial (attention tends to focus on increases). Without errors and omissions, the budget tables needed less time and effort by the central budget staff (analysts appreciate complete budget submissions, which save them much work at an extremely busy time). Cutting back on our own current budget was so shockingly honest and so exceptional that it went a long way toward establishing trust. The massive workload statistics gave credibility to the requests (and gave reassurance to the central budget staff that they could safely approve the requests). Complying so carefully and so completely with the requirements of the budget process added credibility (nothing flatters a bureaucrat more than complete compliance with the system).

All things considered, it was an easy budget to approve. The chief budget analyst proclaimed it "probably the best and most complete budget we have ever received" (an exaggeration, but a very welcome one). The legislative analyst grumbled a bit that the agency must have been overstaffed in the past, but did not pursue the point (it might have suggested a weakness in past budget reviews, as well). The budget request was approved with few changes and little controversy.

Within the department, the reaction was also positive. The commissioner and the managers had been willing to go along with me when I proposed giving up some approved positions and money. After all, I was supposed to know what I was doing. When it worked, it gave them confidence in me. My staff, which had gone along with my demands to make a better budget document, felt good about the results of their added work. As for the additional work I had done personally, I counted it as part of my learning process.

In the years that followed (I think I prepared about three budgets for the department) the trust and cooperation developed that first year carried through. The tactic of cutting back out own budget was a one-time thing, but the benefits were lasting.

The point to all this is that handling the budget (and other administrative services) in a small agency is wonderful experience. "Honest" budgeting is not necessarily better than the traditional game; that may or may not be true, depending on the situation. Administrative service work may not sound very important or stimulating, but in fact it can be satisfying if you see it as a way of supporting the managers of an important public agency and at the same time learning new and useful skills.

When I left, I was sorry to go, even though I had always expected to leave sooner or later. It was a small agency, but full of people and activities with which I had become very familiar. I did not leave because I had learned all I could there, or because I unhappy. I left when I felt I was ready for something more and when I felt that it was probably a choice of leave now or never.

Chapter Three

SUPERVISING

IT IS GOOD to keep more than one career path open if you can, rather than pin all your hopes on one possibility. As soon as I could qualify, I had taken the examinations for Administrative Service Officer II and for Senior Administrative Analyst. I would have taken whichever one had a good opening first.

The first opening – Administrative Service Officer II – was fortunately in San Francisco, but unfortunately in the Fish and Game department. I was unable to present myself convincingly as an avid hunter-fisher and the Director rightly chose someone more compatible.

The next opening was in Sacramento. The Chief Analyst, my former boss, offered me an appointment as Senior Administrative Analyst on his staff in the Finance department. All things considered, it seemed a sort of now-or-never choice: come back to Sacramento now, or not at all.

In one sense it was a matter of coming back to the same kind of work I had done before – making analytical studies for various State agencies and recommending on administrative and management issues. In another sense it would be very different. While I would do some studies personally, the major work was supervising a group of about a half-dozen analysts.

During the three years I had been away, the management analysis staff had mushroomed. It was no longer one small group but a cluster of several units with a hierarchy of its own. I would head one of these units.

State government had also been growing and becoming more complex. The old capitol building itself reflected the change. From the front, its domed wedding-cake civic style looked much the same as always. At the back, however, an enormous block-square concrete office building annex had been attached. It was much larger than the old capitol, and its four-story rather unattractive bulk symbolized the explosive growth of State government.

In another bit of neat symbolism, the old and the new buildings did not fit together very well. To connect the three-story high-ceiling old and the four-story low-ceiling new parts required a maze of passages and stairs. In some places one had to go upstairs to cross over to a lower floor, or vice versa. (Accommodating the new in State government while keeping the old was possible, but not easy.) In my new job, I went to work in one of the hundreds of grey metal-walled offices which lined the long, low windowless corridors of the vast new capitol annex.

The new space was modern, corporate, comfortable and quiet. It was also impersonal and monotonous – unlike the odd little half-circle Victorian space where I had worked before, overlooking the park (that part of the old capitol had been torn down in order to attach the annex). Now, people were shut away from each other – behind closed doors, in private spaces, farther apart. The capitol building no longer felt like a single community. It was no longer easy to feel at home there.

Paradoxically, it was in this mildly depressing building that I entered what was probably the happiest experience of my work life: supervising a close-knit, supportive and highly effective small group. There were six of us. Others came and went from time to time, but this core group stayed together for about three years. What I remember is not so much the specific assignments but the people and the work environment.

It was a satisfying time in State government for people like me. There were problems, but there was confidence that they were solvable and that progress was being made. There was a growing sense of professionalism, and a feeling that in return for our commitment to public service there would be appropriate opportunities and fairness. Career civil servants were generally praised by political leaders, not blamed. Political appointees were often chosen more for their competence than their political service. It was a hopeful time – in retrospect, perhaps we were naive and self-centered as well, but still we were confident and optimistic.

Another favorable aspect of the work environment was the rapid pace of technological innovations. I remember during this period the excitement of attending the first Sacramento presentation on the Univac computer – and of seeing the first gargantuan computer installed in its own air-conditioned wing in the Employment department. IBM and AT&T and other companies were constantly offering us demonstrations of new equipment for office systems. Transportation of all kinds seemed to be getting better, faster and cheaper. I particularly remember the time the Haloid company showed us an experimental process for making copies from a metal plate, using black powder, an electrical charge, and a little handbrush for removing stray particles of powder We thought it was clever but probably impractical; it was the start of the office copying revolution.

In general, we prided ourselves on being skeptical about technology – hard-nosed and resistant to commercial hype. We did discount much of the marketing hype and we did spot sometimes the unmentioned problems or the negative side-effects. More basically, however, we believed in the benefits of change and assumed that in the long run better technology would bring better administration. After all, progressive change was our goal.

Another favorable factor was that by this time the idea of management analysis – get the facts, analyze them, recommend improvements – was more widely known and accepted in State government. There was less need to justify our existence.

At the same time, however, as people had more experience with analysts there was more criticism – not of the theory, but of the practice and the results. Clients were less willing to accept recommendations on faith, simply because they claimed to be objective. They wanted in-depth, accurate fact-finding and specific, up-front support for proposals.

In response, many analysts simply labeled such criticisms as "resistance to change" (as if the problem lay in some faulty tendency of clients to prefer the status quo). There was much searching for sure-fire techniques of overcoming resistance. Actually, clients were often right to resist superficial studies and simplistic proposals. Experienced clients were demanding better work and were pressing analysts to live up to their own promises.

It was a healthy trend which challenged analysts to close the all-too-common gap between theory and practice. It reminded analysts of significant human relationships and values which they had been taught to ignore. It encouraged them to search for better and more sophisticated approaches.

Aside from this generally favorable environment, the specific situation of my analyst group was also fortunate. The people assigned to the group were exceptionally capable and motivated. We were allowed (by the chief analyst and others) a great deal of freedom to work in our own way and given a great deal of support, protection and trust.

The space to which we were assigned happened to be quite separated from the rest of the analysis staff. What might have seemed a disadvantage actually encouraged us to feel a strong group identity and to interact more closely with one another.

All of us shared a strong professional interest in State government and in management analysis. Our backgrounds and abilities differed but tended to complement one another. One was very strong in ability to gain acceptance. Another was our ethical monitor. A third was fascinated with the workings of politics and power, a shrewd observer of who was doing what to whom in the higher ranks. Another had a way of grasping the essentials of complex and difficult issues of public policy. The one who was the most systematic and organized was a reminder that we analysts, too, should be efficient.

As the sixth member of the group (and supervisor) I was particularly able to learn from each, to help them teach one another, and to incorporate something of all of their strengths into my own experience. Ever the generalist, my own greatest strengths were probably still a wide-ranging curiosity and an ability to find unity in diversity.

This assignment was a turning point for me. I learned two things which were extremely useful later on when I became a manager.

First, I learned that working alone and working with others are not two separate ways of working but two aspects of getting any job done. Second, the interpersonal and the technical aspects of administration are similarly interrelated.

Until this time, my job focus had been mainly on myself — doing the job, improving my skills, preparing for advancement. Analytical work can encourage a sort of Lone Ranger mind set: one person, armed with the tools of research, goes where there are problems, gets the facts, analyzes them, solves the problem in the interests of truth, justice and good government, and leaves. You, the Lone Ranger analyst, are in control; others are simply parts of the problem. They are there to give you information and, later on, to accept your solution (with appropriate gratitude). You don't get very involved and you don't stay very long.

As an administrative service officer, relationships with others I worked with were more personal, but I still regarded other people primarily in relation to my own work – as helping or hurting what I was doing. The burden of dealing with others seemed at times a distraction or a side-track from my "real" work – the things I did myself. When I was promoted, I thought of it as primarily the result of my own work, not of what other people had done or as a combined performance.

In leading the analyst group I learned a different approach, one which is more appropriate when most of your work is done through and with others. I had always wanted a lot of freedom and a minimum of control from my supervisors; I could not expect the people in my group to want a heavy-handed boss. They, too, wanted to do it themselves.

Analysts need freedom, but they also need intellectual stimulation, challenge, and continued professional development. They need to be able to kick around problems and possibilities in a safe setting with colleagues who understand the kind of work they are doing. To avoid blind spots and mistakes, it helps to get frank reactions and opinions from people you know and trust.

With these things in mind, I undertook to encourage both clear individual responsibility and free group interaction. I tried to let them develop naturally and gradually, in the course of day-by-day working together.

Here are some of the things which seemed to work:

- Weekly group discussions about management analysis. We agreed on topics in advance and took turns doing the reading and leading the discussions. Sometimes we would work our way through a professional book or journal, taking chapters or articles in turn. The material could be very directly related to work or very broadly related to developments in our field.

- "What's going on" sessions. Traditional staff meetings are routine and dull; the supervisor uses them as a convenient way to give information and instructions or to check on the status of work. In this group, each of us needed to know about current developments in State government, the common context of our work. To feel free to pool our information and to raise questions within the group made for enjoyable and unpredictable sessions.

- Mutual aid. All of us acted at times as consultants, advisers, reviewers, critics, editors, message-takers and spellers for one another. To be asked for this kind of support increases interest; to give it increases capability.

- Work plans. Analysts developed their own work plans for their assignments. The scope, purpose, timing, sources, methods, deadlines, estimated hours, etc. were all put on paper by the person doing the work. Analysts often set higher goals for themselves than a supervisor would impose, and felt more committed to them. As supervisor, my role was to review, not to order. (Often it was to suggest making targets easier, not more difficult.)

- Open office spaces. Actually, I had no choice in this; the assigned space was a common work area plus a small clear-glasses cubicle for me. Some analysts coveted private offices for undisturbed peace and quiet. I preferred that the office function more as a common living room, a base to which we all returned, a place where we kept in touch with one another. Analysts need to spend much of their time out of the office – in temporary space at the agency being studied, in quiet space at the State library or elsewhere (even at home) for sustained reading or writing. Working in such space can sometimes be distracting and even frustrating, but

> in general I would opt for a bit too much togetherness and distraction rather than a bit too much isolation and quiet. The value of learning by overhearing and interacting in a group like this is very great.

If you had looked into this office space, it might have struck you as disorderly, even messy – lots of joking, shop talk, traffic in and out, phones ringing, conversations, work breaks, impromptu get-togethers at one desk or another, questions and answers back and forth. A dynamic group does not have a quiet or orderly space. It thrives in a lively, stimulating, supportive atmosphere in which things just seem to go better than in quieter, more orderly spaces. (To me, an unfortunate side effect of computers in the office is that most of the time they focus people on their monitor screens rather than on other people. The impulse to network by computer and to use phone and fax for a kind of virtual personal contact is healthy, but such technology is not a real substitute for a strong face-to-face informal work group.)

The mention of things seeming to go better reminds me of another quality which I tried for as a supervisor: making it look natural and easy. I worked hard at being a good group leader. I paid attention to details, tried to be sensitive to individuals and to relationships, worried a lot. I also worked very hard not to let the effort show too much and to leave plenty of space for others to make their contributions. My part seemed to work better by example, as a group member. The teamwork needed to be somewhat spontaneous and flexible. I wanted all of us to feel that we did it ourselves (as, in fact, we did).

In such a group, the distinction between work I did myself and the work of others was less clear and less important to me. We each did what we could. Everything contributed to everything. You could not divide it. As a group we probably performed better than we could have alone (I know I did). As group leader, I benefited as much from what others did as from what I did myself. I did not feel I had to be smarter, better and more productive than others. The smarter, better and more productive the group was, the more all of us would benefit (especially me). I suppose you could say that this was merely enlightened self-interest – a different way of being competitive and ultimately self-centered. Perhaps so, but at least the self-interest was enlightened, the competition encouraged everyone to win, and the self-interest included others.

I am not saying that this particular style of group leadership would always be used. It worked well for me in this situation with these people. I have seen bright and able people become poor supervisors or managers because they cannot get beyond their initial work skills. They still need to do everything, to show they can do everything the best, to control everything. They expect to win by competing against and holding down their own subordinates. I spell out an alternative possibility which is less traditional, less obvious, less known. It worked well for me – but, let me emphasize, not all the time. Sometimes I behaved very traditionally – controlled, gave orders, directed, evaluated – and I do not feel guilty or apologetic about that. One style never fits all circumstances. One needs to have in mind, however, some kind of personal preference or ideal. This was mine.

The second area in which I learned a lot at this time was how to get better results from administrative surveys by relating to clients in a different way. In the Insurance department work I had learned how important feelings are. It seemed time to add to the fact-finding and the analysis a larger component of collaboration.

"Participation" is by now an administrative cure-all and cliché: if you let people feel they are "participating" they will follow you anywhere. There is a little truth in this, but not much. Participation is not a method of control. Nor is it a cop-out: find out what the client wants and recommend it. Sometimes the two are used together: make sure you give the managers what they want, and make sure the rank-and-file are made to want what they get. It was enough to give "participation" a bad name with analysts.

What was needed was a participation process which preserved the values of independent inquiry, but improved results. If one shifted perspective a little, participation could be as integral a part of the process in every stage as fact-finding and analysis. At every step of a study, the process needs to allow a wide range of insights and opinions to surface. Everyone affected needs to be thought of as part of the study process, as a potential partner in the study. Instead of controlling the subjects of a study like rats in a research maze, an analyst needs to be truly open to the concerns and contributions of the people involved – in a sense, the rats need to become partners in the research.

In this approach, analysts should be willing to suspend judgment and to revise conclusions on the basis of insights from any source. The concerns of those affected are a proper element in the development of solutions. The study process does not belong only to the analyst. Ideally, in an open process, the people involved would be prepared to implement the results before a report is issued. The report would merely record and publish results, not be the major product of the study.

By this time, such a collaborative approach was widely used by management consulting firms. In State government, however, the central analyst staff still practiced the traditional arms-length "independent" study (perhaps because the chief analyst was a former auditor). Fortunately, our group was allowed latitude in deciding how to do our work. We had to meet the requirement of a carefully written, fully documented, standard-format report at the end of each study, but were not prevented from conducting the studies in full partnership with the client agencies. If the success rate improved, our management was certainly going to be pleased. If not, the fault would be ours.

A few quick illustrations of the newer approach may clarify the differences:

- The analyst should become in effect a temporary part of the organization under study, not merely an outside observer.

- The feelings and relationships of people are "facts," too, as important to a study as the formal structures and processes.

- The analyst needs to develop mutual trust and respect with the other people involved, not merely remain remote and objective.

- Solutions have to be fitted specifically to the particular circumstances, not based on generalities.

- The impact of changes on people is important.

- Solutions in which everyone's needs are met are worth the added effort.

- The analyst should be both an "inside" catalyst, counselor and facilitator and an "outside" analyst, specialist and critic.

With this approach, the extent to which our studies were implemented did increase. Our superiors were pleased that so often we could report that all concerned agreed with the results of a study (or, better yet, sometimes – that the proposals had already been put into action). Happiness for an administrative analyst is being able to reach such agreement, honestly and openly.

At the same time that our group was getting such good results by increased collaboration with clients, the over-all policy of the chief analyst was moving in a somewhat opposite direction. As State government continued to grow, many of the larger departments wanted to have their own budget, personnel, purchasing, and other staff administrative services. The central staffs often encouraged these departmental outposts because they tended to work in partnership with their central counterparts, who remained in over-all control.

The situation for management analysis evolved very differently. The chief analyst was convinced that departments should not be allowed to have management analysts, and that all work should be done by his office for all State agencies. For him, the crucial issue was independence and objectivity; he believed that such positions would be misused and manipulated in departments. The departments, however, saw it as depriving them of an adequate service and forcing them to rely on a remote Finance-controlled central staff. The chief analyst could influence the budget process and sometimes could prevent agencies from getting management analyst positions; other agencies, particularly the larger ones, sometimes got them approved. There were also arguments over the level of analyst positions, which the central Personnel agency controlled. The chief analyst, if unable to prevent the positions from being established, tried to keep them at a lower level than the positions on his own staff. These conflicts between the chief analyst and the departments also impaired relations between central and departmental analysts. Under the circumstances, there was little basis for mutual cooperation and support.

Unlike the budget, personnel, and purchasing systems, there was no common process or work cycle which linked the departmental and central analysts in a common system. Once departments got analysts, they stopped asking the central staff to study what they regarded as primarily departmental matters and used their analysts as they chose. The central staff did more of its work for other central agencies, especially for the central budget staff, and was seen by departments as becoming an instrument of centralized control (particularly, since the chief analyst now reported to the chief budget officer rather than to the Director of Finance).

The gap between the central and the departmental analyst staffs was increasing. Both were growing, but separately and in opposition to one another.

I found myself increasingly at odds with my own office on these issues. I felt that departments should be encouraged to have analyst staffs and that the central analyst staff should work in partnership with them to improve State government. There were opportunities (for training, for cooperation, for movement of analysts among agencies, for improving the use of management analysts) which were being wasted. I liked very much the work I was doing, but I did not want to find myself isolated in a few years within a limited central staff doing a narrowing range of work. I liked both central and departmental staff work and wanted to keep my options open in both directions.

Because of these feelings, I did work with a number of other management analysts to establish a local professional society, the Systems and Procedures Association, an unofficial and voluntary organization open to all management analysts in State government and to those in Federal and private organizations, as well. It provided a social meeting place, sponsored some training, and was to some extent a forum for discussing common concerns. Most central and departmental analysts in State government, however, showed little interest and did not participate. The effort did not have any major or lasting effect. The gap between the central and the departmental management analyst functions remained an unsolved problem of State organization and administration (Physician, heal thyself!)

Chapter Four

DEVELOPING A MANAGEMENT PROGRAM

THE HEAD OF the San Francisco Port Commission, Cyril Magnin, helped me become a manager. He did it inadvertently, by asking the Director of Finance to approve the hiring of a management consulting firm to study Port administration.

The Port's shipping operations were declining and its real estate operations were growing. It controlled among other things the land under Fisherman's Wharf, a major tourist attraction. Other California ports were operated by local governments. The San Francisco Embarcadero had been developed by State financing, the State owned the land, and the Port was under State control at that time, even though the State no longer provided any money. The Commission was somewhat restless about being a State agency and wanted an independent evaluation of how the Port should be organized and managed.

The Director of Finance agreed that such a study was a good idea, but made a counter-proposal: the Port need not hire a consulting firm; the Finance Department's analyst staff would do the survey at no cost to the Port. Magnin agreed. I was assigned to head the project and given three other analysts.

The Director of Finance misled Mr. Magnin a little, implying that this was the sort of study his analyst staff did all the time. He probably wanted to accommodate Magnin's interest in administration, to save money, and to have the work done by his own staff rather than by a private firm chosen by the Port Commission.

Actually, the study was a great deal larger and broader and more complex than anything the analyst staff had done before. It was the first time we had been invited to take a look at every aspect of the administration of such a large State agency — everything from broad policies to minor details. It was also the first study which required such a large task force (instead of the usual one-person one-project assignments). The Port itself was unique: a State-owned but quasi-local public utility, operating a major transportation service, leasing out waterfront land for commercial use, even operating a small dock-side freight railroad.

None of our analyst group knew anything about port administration in general or the San Francisco Port in particular, but we knew that Magnin, an experienced and successful businessman, would be expecting a quality job. So would the Director of Finance. So would the Chief Administrative Analyst.

There were, one might say, some risks as well as some opportunities for all concerned with the project. Nevertheless, Magnin agreed wholeheartedly with the plan, pledged his personal support, and got us off to a good start with the Port director and staff.

The study was done in San Francisco over a period of about four months. I continued to lead my regular group about one day a week in Sacramento and spent the rest of my work time (and more) with the project team.

In the long run what was important to me was not what we recommended but how it was received. We covered everything from the name of the agency and who should own it (the State) to its marketing, real estate management, finances, accounting, organization and staffing. It was generally well received by the Port managers. Our main client, Cyril Magnin, was wonderfully generous. He praised our work highly and let the Director of Finance know he was pleased.

I don't really know how much of the report was put into effect by the San Francisco Port. When the report was completed and delivered I returned to Sacramento and to other project assignments. As it happened, however, the Director of the State Department of Public Works was deciding at about this time to establish an administrative analyst position in his office, to develop an administrative analysis program in this large State agency.

The Director of Public Works had not expected to find the person be wanted for this position within State service. He had insisted that the examination be open to anyone in California. There were many applicants and a lengthy examination process, both written and oral. Fortunately, I came out at the top of the list. The Director did not have to choose me (the next two on the list were from outside State government), but he had to choose among the top three candidates.

It was the just-completed San Francisco Port study which made the crucial difference in my favor (other factors being somewhat equal). The Director read the report and liked it. He saw the Port (concerned with transportation and real estate) as somewhat similar to his own agency (concerned with highway transportation and State building construction). I assume he also contacted Magnin and the Director of Finance, who were blue-ribbon personal references for me. It was enough. I got the job.

There were a few other lucky breaks along the way. As usual, the Chief Administrative Analyst opposed having an analyst position established anywhere except on his own staff. He tried to get the proposed position disapproved, but was unsuccessful. The Director of Public Works headed one of the most important State agencies. He was not only able to get the position budgeted but to get it approved as a Supervising Administrative Analyst, a higher level than had been approved anywhere outside the Department of Finance at that time. It was a major promotion from my previous position.

As I left the Department of Finance (for the second and last time), the Chief Administrative Analyst wished me well, but made it plain he thought I should not be leaving his staff again, that the job I was taking should not have been established, that it was at far too high a level, and that the whole thing was a big mistake. Nevertheless, I am sure he must have given me a favorable personal recommendation. He could not block the creation of the job, but he did not block my promotion to it, for which I was grateful. It seemed very clear, however, that from here on I would be on my own as far as he was concerned.

I did wonder whether the chief analyst appreciated the irony: by giving me the Port assignment, he had made it possible for me to do exactly what he did not want me to do, to strike out on my own. I appreciated all he had done to help me learn, but I felt it was time to go, that I was ready to do more than I could do as part of his staff. For nine years he had been patient and protective, even when he must have thought me a bit of a smart-ass for my frank opinions and open disagreements with some of his ideas. It was lucky that I could leave for such an attractive opportunity and promotion, but one way or another I would probably have left soon anyway. A mentor can be very helpful, but may also want to keep you in what the mentor thinks of as "your place."

Looking at the Department of Public Works, I felt that the challenge of the Port study (a small team undertaking to analyze a large and unfamiliar agency) was small compared to what my new post involved: one person undertaking to establish and lead a new program in a huge and complex State bureaucracy.

I did know something about the Department, but not much. Before I took the appointment I had done some checking. It was obvious that Public Works was a long-established, independent, proud, conservative and somewhat arrogant organization, protected by powerful legislators, construction-minded governors, construction-hungry lobby groups, reliable and growing Federal and State financing, and a system of laws which insulated it from what the department would have regarded as outside interference.

What was not as obvious was what contribution I could make to this organization as a management analyst – or even what had really caused the Director suddenly to want one of them on his staff. I assumed he must have something in mind, assured myself that I could do whatever it was he wanted, and accepted the job offer with enthusiasm.

It took less than two weeks on the job to find out the truth: he really didn't have anything specific in mind for me to do. He just felt that the idea of management analysis was good and that I would find some way to be useful and improve the management of the agency. At this point, I wondered if I had won an opportunity or buried a career.

I began to feel the shock of reality the very first day. I marched through the green-marble lobby, across the spacious reception room, through the polished oak double-doors, into the walnut-paneled carpeted executive suite to the desk of the Director's secretary. She informed me pleasantly that (1) my office was out the double-doors and down the hall past the mail room and past the file room and around the corner, (2) I must never use paper clips (against office rules – they might catch papers on one another), and (3) the Director wanted to see me right away.

The Director's greeting was friendly and brisk. Instead of asking me to sit on one of the massive leather chairs so we could chat across his huge carved-wood desk (as I had expected), he bounced out of his swivel chair and announced that he was taking me on a tour of the building to meet a few people. In half an hour of fast walking and brief talking, he introduced me to the State Highway Engineer, the State Architect, the State Water Engineer, and the Chief of the Contracts and Rights of Way (Legal) Division.

Except for the Director's immediate staff, nearly everyone in this huge department worked in one of the divisions headed by these four men. At each of the four offices I got a handshake, a quick welcome, and a clear instruction to contact him (or his chief deputy) if I needed anything. In other words, stick to channels and don't come into my territory without my permission.

When we got back to his office, the Director expressed confidence that I would find useful things to do, said something like "good luck," shook my hand and disappeared into his office. I departed to find my cubbyhole, wondering what it all had meant.

Later in the day, each of the two deputy directors explained in his own way what was going on. The political deputy told me the reason I was there was that neither he nor his close friend (the personnel officer) had been able to get through the protective walls and into the divisions (particularly, they wanted access to the largest and most important, the Highways division) They hoped that a management analyst would somehow get into the divisions and then bring back to them what they expected would be evidence of poor management. This deputy said he was the one who had persuaded the Director to set up my job. He said that I should let him and his friend, the personnel officer, know everything I did and everything I found. He wished me luck.

The career deputy, a long-time civil servant who had risen through the ranks, warned me to beware of the political deputy and the personnel officer. He said that the divisions were deeply suspicious of their motives and that if the divisions felt I was part of their team I would never be trusted. He suggested I have as little as possible to do with them. He also said that there would not be much for me to do unless I could somehow get access to the divisions, especially the Highways division. The Director's main administrative work was approving State construction contracts, which the career deputy handled. Except for a few personnel matters, practically everything else had long since been delegated to the divisions or had been taken over by them.

The Director's position was powerful, he explained, only because he chaired the Highway Commission, the Toll Bridge Authority, and the Public Works Board, which set policy and approved financing for State construction projects. As Director, he actually exercised little control over administration or management of the agency, which was left largely to the divisions. The Director had taken me around personally on that tour as a symbolic gesture of support – and because it was about the only thing he could do to help me get started. Beyond that, the career deputy said, I would have to figure out what to do and how to get the confidence of the division heads and their staffs. He wished me luck.

As it turned out, there were some more things the Director could do to help me, once I figured out how to work within the situation. First, I drafted and he signed a letter to all the division heads announcing my appointment, describing generally the kind of work I would be doing, and encouraging them to talk with me about possible assignments for their divisions. The memo emphasized that in any work I did for a division I would be in effect a member of their staff and would present the results directly to the division.

It was a further expression of support, bureaucratically correct, and a step toward my first three goals: to explain what I could do to help people, to begin to establish personal trust, and to avoid becoming entangled in bureaucratic politics.

I really didn't expect any response from the divisions to the Director's memo about me – nothing positive and nothing negative – and that's what I got. At this early stage no response was a good response. Meanwhile, I needed some immediate work. I chose two things as appropriate vehicles: (1) the removal from the Public Works Department of the Water Resources division (part of the Governor's and the Legislature's plan to undertake construction of the California Water Project), and (2) the general lack of understanding of the concept of management analysis. The first gave me an opportunity to prepare a new updated chart of the Public Works Department for the Director. The second provided a basis for developing a written statement of what I hoped would become a management analysis program – what kind of work I would be doing and how it would be done.

These early undertakings fit the bureaucratic traditions of the agency (acting in the name of the director, putting it in writing, respecting the delegated authority of the divisions), but to me they were immediate and practical. What I needed was some non-controversial work which would enable me to talk one-to-one with as many of the top officials of the divisions as possible. I needed the process more than the products.

Organization charts are always important to executives, particularly in a bureaucracy. The way charts are drawn (which involves many choices) can show positions to advantage or disadvantage, making them look more important or less important. Naturally, division heads would be interested in talking with me about a new chart (and in the process about their jobs and their place in the organization.)

Drawing charts fairly and clearly showed technical competence. It showed also that I was working closely with the Director and other top officials. The conversations it triggered were helpful. (It is a good starting move: if in doubt, suggest the need for an updated organization chart; the current one is almost always somewhat out of date.)

The project to develop a statement of the management analysis program for the department was much more difficult and much more important. It made sense to clarify for others something which was then only a vision in my head. Division heads were not about to invite me into their organizations, but if I offered to talk with them and with people in their divisions to get their reaction to a policy draft they could hardly refuse or object.

I was offering them a reassuring amount of control by implicitly accepting my need for their approval of the eventual final product. In return I had a chance to explain my intentions and interests and to find ways to meet both their needs and mine. It was a useful two-way process which I was in no hurry to complete as long as it was helping all of us to learn. (Also there was a sort of subtext: there really is going to be a management analysis program and here is what it will do and how it will work. In a large bureaucracy, nothing confirms the virtual reality of a new program more quickly than a policy directive from the chief executive.)

When the Director eventually approved and signed the policy statement and made it official, the action was almost an anticlimax. As I had hoped, it was by that time non-controversial. Nobody was surprised. Nobody was upset. It did commit me to certain ways of operating, but the self-imposed limitations were the way I would have operated anyway. Most people probably remained skeptical or unimpressed or uninterested, but on paper at least the program now had official status, identity and visibility – useful qualities in a large organization. It "existed." Now it just needed to become real.

The most important "limitation" was tailored to the situation in the department: I was part of the Director's staff, but most of the work I wanted to do was in the divisions. The divisions did not want to let the Director's office get involved in their internal affairs; I could not work on most administrative matters without getting into division operations. The solution: I would work directly for any official who asked for a study – in some cases, for the Director, in other cases (I hoped) for a division head (or whomever the division head designated). In other words, as a management consultant, I would work directly with each client. The Director would approve my doing a project for a division, but from then on I would in effect be a temporary addition to the division staff. I was offering a free in-house management consulting service for potential clients throughout the agency – and all within the rules of bureaucratically correct channels.

This one arrangement made the new program possible. Getting agreement on it at the start (before any controversy had arisen) was not difficult. The divisions had no reason to object: it gave them the control they wanted. 'The Director was comfortable with it: he just wanted me to find useful work and trusted me that this was the appropriate way to do it; if he should want me to do something, I was available. The political deputy did not object: I convinced him that only in this way could I have access to the divisions.

I did not mind offering to report at a "lower" level part of the time. The usual bureaucratic idea is always to report at the "highest" possible level in the organization, to maximize power and prestige. In this case, I needed freedom to work in whatever way fit the project and the situation. Only by escaping from the Director's Office part of the time could I hope to do what I needed to do. Also I was sending a useful message: I am not looking for personal power and prestige.

At that point, a month or two into the job, the program was on paper but still nobody was asking me to do anything. It was the political deputy who unexpectedly came up with an assignment which could have been either a big mistake or a big opportunity.

He came into my office one day with a wide grin and said something like, "John, I've just worked out a wonderful deal for you." He explained that the powerful Senate Interim Committee on Public Works was forming a task force to study right-of-way administration in the Highways division. A team of management analysts loaned for several months from private corporations would do the work for the Committee, which was the major legislative group dealing with the highway program. It was obviously an important study — important to the legislature, the department, the Highways division, and the highway program.

What the political deputy had seen was an opportunity to get me inside the Highways division and inside one of its major and growing components. What he had done was arrange for me to be a member of the task force. What he expected was that I would bring him word of what was really going on inside the Highways division. What I instantly felt was a mixture of pleasure and dismay. It was one of those defining moments which can take you so totally by surprise.

Let me explain my mixed feelings. This could indeed be the start-up opportunity I needed. The deputy had it right: Highways division could not keep me out if I were part of such a group and they could not properly object to the assignment (and anyway, he explained, it was all settled).

The dismaying part was what seemed clear to me: later on, the way he had set it up would not work. I would be caught in an incompatible situation – expected to act as agent and informant for the political deputy, tied to an unknown group of analysts on a politically sponsored task force of unknown motivation or competence, forced eventually either to support or dissent from whatever findings and proposals the task force might develop, likely to be seen by Highways division officials as a political opportunist who could not be trusted. I would surely wind up in big trouble, one way or another.

The deputy was not offering me the choice of accepting or refusing the deal. It was done. However, thinking back to the management analysis policy statement which had been issued, I saw a third possibility. If the deputy would be a little flexible, the deal could be accepted – but modified.

I thanked the deputy for his great idea, said I would be glad to work with the task force, but urged him to go back to his legislative contacts and get one "small" change in the terms of my assignment: instead of being a full-fledged member of the task force, I would work with them as liaison for the Public Works department. I would still be assigned full-time, as he had arranged. I would travel with them, help them, see that they got the information they needed, participate fully in their survey work, but (crucial difference) I would not participate in the development of their conclusions and recommendations. One other thing: I wanted to talk with the State Highway Engineer about the arrangement before it was announced.

The deputy was not very pleased with what he saw as my tinkering with his arrangements. He did not like the idea of going back to revise a deal he had just made. I argued, however, that unless we modified the plan I might wind up being involved in legislative matters which as political deputy were his business, not mine. As a task force member I might be committed to support positions to which he and the department were opposed. Reluctantly, he agreed to go back. As I had suspected, it turned out to be easy to get the arrangement changed. The task force head was happy to have my help, but was glad not to have a stranger from the department thrust upon him as a full member of the task force.

When I met with the State Highway Engineer, I told him everything: how the proposed arrangement had arisen and how it had been modified. I offered to keep him currently and fully briefed on task force activities. In effect, I explained, I would be working as the policy required, operating as a member of his staff to help make the study accurate and useful and to see that he was not caught by surprise. He readily agreed to the arrangement and said he would be available whenever I needed to talk with him.

Bingo! Suddenly I had what I needed – step two: a chance to prove myself in action, with a flexible arrangement which met everyone's needs and expectations without putting me into conflict with anyone.

The point here, I believe, is not the luck of being able to turn an unexpected event to advantage, but the advantage of having thought carefully about what you might do if the unexpected does happen. An immediate response is likely to be better with the benefit of such preparation – "if this happens, do this" or "to get this result, do this." It helps to have thought in advance; that's really all that "policy" is, advance guidelines for actions and decisions. (This can work both for organizations and individuals.)

During the next three months, the assignment worked out as planned. Working full-time with the task force, I went through all the major units of the division headquarters and traveled with the group to several of the eleven district offices. I learned a great deal and became fairly widely acquainted. Everywhere, I marketed myself and my program.

The industry analysts (loaned by their companies) turned out to be competent professionals who wanted to do a good straightforward job and show some practical results, so their companies would think well of their efforts. Their only concern had been that they might find themselves involved in politics. As professional analysts, we found that we had much in common.

As liaison, I was able to be genuinely helpful. I saw to it that people in Highways understood what the task force was trying to do and what information they needed. I was also able to help the business-oriented task force understand State government, interpret accurately the attitudes of the division, and shape recommendations in ways most likely to be accepted by the division.

From the beginning, the task force was aware of my commitment to keep the department and division executives informed about the study. Fortunately, they understood that these contacts would also help the task force – increase understanding, reduce apprehensions, improve the chances of a successful outcome for the study.

For me, the opportunity to meet frequently and privately with the State Highway Engineer over a period of several months was most important. We got to know each other. He proved to be a canny, tough old administrator (everyone over fifty seemed old to me then) whom I respected. I think I was a different sort of young person than he was used to; in his strongly hierarchical division it would take thirty years for a junior engineer to reach this level of open and informal discussion with him. I was a sort of novelty, I think, and he seemed increasingly to like and trust me.

The task force report satisfied the legislative committee and satisfied the department and division as well. It proposed some administrative improvements and some changes in legislation (which is what the committee wanted) but also praised many aspects of the present operations (which is what the division wanted). The changes were generally acceptable and many were eventually put into effect.

I do not want to imply that my part in all this was important. I was a newcomer, a minor staff employee, and a very small part of a very large situation. I was very far from being able to control the course of events. I felt satisfied that I had done what I could, had done it well, had helped things go better, had helped myself, and had put my good luck to good use. What more could you expect?

When it was all over, the State Highway Engineer let me in on his little secret. I remarked that I had tried to be completely honest and accurate in briefing him about the study. He puffed on his pipe a bit, came as near to smiling as he ever did, and said something like, "I'm sure you always told me the truth because I had another source inside that task force. I knew you were being honest with me. I would have known immediately if you hadn't been."

How naive of me, I thought, not to have guessed. He would not have risked depending only on my information. He was testing me all the time. Lucky that I had played it straight. (In complex situations, I believe that honesty can be a most effective – and surprising – strategy, especially if you feel comfortable with it.)

From then on, the State Highway Engineer trusted me. Within a few months, I was able (with his approval and support) to work within the division and to develop projects and assignments with his staff. I had passed some sort of test and it made all the difference.

The next step in developing the management analysis program was to identify a project which would be (1) useful to the division in solving a real problem, (2) non-threatening and compatible with the division's ways of operating, (3) appropriate for a management analyst, (4) something I could do, and (5) if possible, something which could be extended later to other parts of the department. During my travels with the task force, I found a problem which fit all of these criteria: records management.

The Highways division had been accumulating huge quantities of paper records of all sorts, ever since the 1920's – correspondence, engineering drawings, construction records, maintenance records, property records, etc.. For a long time, it had been just a matter of adding file equipment and space, but now with the rapid growth of the Interstate Highway System program it was becoming an expensive headache – not only in terms of added space and equipment, but in terms of simply keeping track of and finding needed records. As in most large organizations at the time, there had been no overall plan for management of the records – no planning of where to keep them, how to store them, when to dispose of them, how to make them useful and efficient as part of an information system. What had long been neglected as mere clerical routine had become a real administrative problem suitable for a management analysis study and solvable without threatening anyone (a real "win-win" project).

In the Department of Finance, I had worked closely with an analyst who had established the general outlines of a records management program for State government. She had already helped several State departments bring their records systems under control. With her years of State service in supervising file systems and her professional training in records management, I knew that she had the blend of tact, empathy and skill which would enable her to establish a records management system for the Highways division. (Another possible principle: don't do it yourself if somebody else can do it better.)

Using the already-adopted management analysis policy, I talked with the State Highway Engineer and with the aides who were most concerned with the growth of records. I obtained their agreement that the problem was serious, that it was getting worse, and that nobody was dealing with it on a division-wide basis. I offered to help by bringing in an analyst skilled and experienced in records management if they would authorize the position.

This was a part of a larger step: establishing a management analysis unit in the Highways division. I offered to work within the division on a nearly full-time basis to head the new unit. I would report in this role to the State Highway Engineer through one of his administrative deputies. It would be a continuing program. The records project alone would take several years. Other studies of organization and procedure would be undertaken for the division. I suggested and got approval for two analyst positions plus a secretary, with the understanding that as workload increased more analysts would be added. My friend and co-worker from the Finance Department, attracted by the chance to work in a new and developing program, accepted a transfer to become the first division analyst hired.

A key factor in getting approval for all this was the unconventional and (from a bureaucratic standpoint) somewhat amusing idea that I would be holding two similar but distinctly different jobs at the same time in the same hierarchy – one as analyst in the Director's office and the other (the new position) as analyst heading a staff in the Highways division.

To the division officials, I pointed out that the departmental policy authorized my working in the division on assignments. It did not say how long an assignment could last, and if it turned out to be 10 or 20 years or so, that would be alright (so long as all concerned were happy with the arrangement).

To the Director, I emphasized that this was a way (perhaps a little unorthodox, but a feasible way) for me to work within the division and do the kind of work for which he had hired me. Anticipating that he (and his two deputies) might worry that I would no longer be available to help them in the Director's office, I proposed that an analyst be hired as my assistant there.

It worked. Suddenly instead of just myself and an uncertain future I had two staffs and three analysts and a secretary and the ability to move flexibly between my first-floor departmental cubbyhole and my division office on the second floor. To me, both were aspects of a single evolving program. To each of my two superiors, I was still available to direct the work in which he was interested.

The arrangement might seem to violate a so-called principle of administration (one which is so ancient it is even given in the Bible's Old Testament): you cannot serve two masters. Many people in organizations, however, do in fact take orders from more than one person without problems. The fuller and more accurate maxim is this: if you are subject to orders from more than one person, there needs to be an agreed-upon way to resolve conflicting orders. I felt that under the circumstances I could satisfy both bosses; there should be conflicting instructions, the Director would be the ultimate authority. (The proverbs of good administration are over-simplified and need to be used creatively to fit specific situations. The real questions are "Does it work well?" and "Is it the best feasible arrangement under the circumstances?")

In this case, the answer to both questions was clearly "yes." Both parts of the program soon took root and began to thrive. My dual "identity" became familiar to all concerned. I even found myself sometimes writing letters from one of my "selves" to the other or from one of my bosses to the other. Coordination between the two analysis units was easy – it took place in my head.

It was fortunate that the program developed so rapidly. Just about the time it was going well – perhaps six months after I had arrived – I received a copy of a management analysis study published by the Finance Department staff where I used to work. It suddenly reminded me that the Chief Analyst's fixed idea was that analyst positions in departments should be (1) prevented, (2) eliminated, or (3) held to a low pay level (so that the Finance department analyst staff would be the only service for all State agencies). The report urged that this idea be adopted as policy.

Worse, the report singled out my Supervising Administrative Analyst position for particular criticism. It proposed that my position be downgraded (because, it said, I did not have supervisory responsibilities) and said that I should be demoted. It was unusual for the Finance analyst staff to recommend on the level of positions (usually handled by the State Personnel Board), particularly a class of positions where the conflict of interest was so obvious, but the recommendation was buried inside a massive report of an over-all study of the whole Department of Finance. It was also unusual that my former associates had not bothered to check recent developments and were unaware that I now supervised a staff of five.

I wrote to the Finance department a polite but angry memo over my own signature, pointing out to my former boss (a stickler for accuracy) the factual errors. I told him that I had never been contacted during the "study" and emphasized that I would have been happy to cooperate with a policy review but would not accept an unfounded personal attack based on inaccurate information. There was no reply. Nothing more was heard about this particular recommendation.

There was one funny footnote to this episode. A few days after I had sent my letter to the Department of Finance I was warmly congratulated on it by the State Highway Engineer and his chief deputy (to whom I had sent an information copy). The Highways division was independent in most respects from budgetary and administrative control by the Finance department (its money being mostly allocated directly from State highway revenues by State highway laws). Highway officials did, however, respect the power of the Finance department and usually avoided conflict with it. They enjoyed tremendously my very personal and very direct letter. They recognized the anger beneath the politeness. To them it was an act of courage (which was not true — I was just angry). They also took it as a further demonstration that my loyalty and commitment were no longer to the Finance department but to the Public Works department and the Highways division (which was true — and had been true since the day I arrived).

Chapter Five

AIDE TO A MANAGER

THERE IS A good deal of difference between directing a program and being an aide to a manager – and changing over involved some risks and some opportunities.

By this time (about 1958) the new management analysis program which I had established in the Department of Public Works was three years old and doing well. Outside political events, however, were about to change my situation and my role.

Most of the management analysis program was being done in the Highways division. I was spending most of my time there. The concepts of in-house analytical studies – objective studies, applying accepted principles, making recommendations, writing reports – were all compatible with engineering concepts. Once assured that there was not a political motive or an attempt at "outside" interference, there was increasing acceptance and more requests for studies. (From an analyst's point of view, engineers tend to be good clients. They like to deal in terms of factual data and rational analysis.)

The records management program got particularly good results. It was eventually the subject of a major article in the widely-circulated in-house department magazine, *California Highways and Public Works.* (A photograph with the article showed graphically, in terms of "ghost" file cabinets, the cubic feet of office space and equipment saved to date.)

At the same time, I continued to keep in touch with the Director and his staff enough to remain part of that group, as well. With the help of a very capable analyst, the Director's office received the services they needed – analyzing proposed legislation, compiling administrative policies, and reviewing procedures.

From the administrative deputy and the lawyers I learned enough about construction contracting to sign such documents when the Director and the deputy were away. I was given a full delegation of authority to act on their behalf. I used it only occasionally, when back-up was needed, but it was a significant authorization. As a matter of principle such authority was not granted to anyone outside the Director's office. With the help of the attorneys, the Director used this as a final check on the letting of contracts under the State Contract Act. Hundreds of millions worth of construction projects were handled under this process with integrity and reliability

During this time, I also began teaching public administration at Sacramento State College (later, California State University, Sacramento). For the convenience of working students (and practitioner faculty), these were taught in the evening but were part of the regular undergraduate and graduate degree programs of the political science department. Many of the students were already working in State government, or hoped to do so. The public administration programs used some State administrators as part-time teachers along with the core of regular full-time teachers. I started with administrative analysis and moved on to introductory public administration and other topics, but always limited my teaching to one semester a year, so as not to interfere with my full-time State work.

In late 1958 and early 1959, this stable, balanced and satisfying work pattern was suddenly interrupted by outside political events. In 1958, Edmund (Pat) Brown was elected Governor. The Republican Party had seriously wounded itself by forcing Governor Goodwin Knight to run for U.S. Senator and allowing Senator Knowland to run for Governor. Knight had been Lieutenant Governor with Warren. When Warren was appointed to the U.S. Supreme Court, Knight had continued much of Warren's moderate and somewhat bi-partisan policies with considerable success. Confronted with this unexpected shuffling of candidates, the majority of voters turned instead to the Democratic candidate, who had been State Attorney General (an elective office in California). There had been only one Democratic governor in California for decades. Brown's victory was a major political event, the first partisan turn-over since before World War II.

The initial impact on me personally began during the period between the November election of Brown and his January inauguration as Governor. Suddenly, there were only a few of us left in the Director's office. The political deputy (who had succeeded in becoming Director along the way) resigned for an appointment to a new Metropolitan Transit agency in Southern California. The administrative deputy had been killed in an auto accident earlier that year and had not yet been replaced. The personnel officer had died of a heart attack while playing tennis in the Sacramento heat. The assistant director, a former local government official whose job was liaison with local governments regarding highway matters, was appointed interim Director to finish out the year. He appointed me an assistant director on a temporary basis to help keep the office going until the end of the year by handling much of the contracting and administrative work.

This short-term caretaker role would clearly last only until incoming Governor Brown appointed a new Director. However, it did establish me at least temporarily in an executive position. In preparation for the arrival of new leadership we reorganized the office and, among other things made the Assistant Director of Public Works a civil service position (to which, if successful in a competitive examination, the acting Director would be eligible for appointment).

Later on, I took this Assistant Director exam, but with the understanding that if successful I would "go inactive," meaning that I would not be available for appointment. With my State experience and veteran's preference, I did in fact rank high on the list after the open competitive exam. I went inactive, as planned, and eventually the new Director did appoint the former acting Director to this career civil service position.

After that, I put my name back on the active list. If there should be another vacancy for an Assistant Director of Public Works during the next two or three years, I would be one of three people at the top of the list who could be considered for appointment.

I had no idea whether the opportunity would arise. I did not know who my next bosses would be. I was following some personal "rules" about how to work with the State personnel system:

1. Take any exams for which you are eligible if, sooner or later, you might conceivably be interested in the job;

2. Understand the civil service rules, so you will know how to use them appropriately for your purposes;

3. Make it easy to be appointed under civil service (but recognize that many factors other than the examinations will enter into the appointment decisions, and that they are unpredictable).

In other words, look out for yourself, know the system, plan ahead, and be realistic and patient. Not a bad system, especially if you do well on written and oral examinations.

When Governor Brown appointed a new Director of Public Works and a new political deputy, it was immediately clear to me that my convenient little dual-role system would have to go. The new director was a seasoned Federal executive with experience in heading large public agencies and programs. The new political deputy was an "insider" on the new Governor's political team, well placed to link this large and important department with the new central administration. Soon, a new administrative deputy was also appointed – exempt from civil service, but an experienced city manager with good professional qualifications.

Clearly this was a different kind of team which would expect a different kind of assistance from me, as the departmental administrative analyst. In contrast to the previous situation, the Director's office would be an active center of over-all executive and political energy and authority. An administrative analyst who spent most of his time off somewhere in the Highways division doing things for them would not be likely to appeal to my new bosses as a useful or necessary part of the Director's office.

Before the issue arose, I set about at my own initiative to reverse the arrangements I myself had made. It was a new situation, one which called for a new solution. I explained to the new Director and deputies as soon as they arrived that (1) I had been working mostly in Highways, (2) I was willing, able and eager to shift and spend my time helping them, and (3) I could particularly help them initially with State administrative systems, rules and practices, from the standpoint of a career civil servant.

Meanwhile, I explained my new situation to the State Highway Engineer and his deputies and said that I could no longer handle both jobs. Through them I set in motion the process for holding a civil service examination for a full-time analyst to head the division analysis staff there (in place of my division assignment).

I hoped very much that the analyst who headed the records management program would be appointed. She had done an outstanding job and deserved to be promoted. With our experience in working together, I felt that we could continue the informal coordination between the department and division which had been so useful for all concerned.

Unfortunately, it did not turn out that way. While one can to some extent influence the civil service exam process (by advising on the scope of the written exam and being a member of the oral exam group), one cannot (and should not) control it.

I had seriously misjudged what would happen. Although she had a fine record of successful work performance, she did not have a college degree (education and experience were technically interchangeable, but in professional administrative exams an academic credential was an advantage). Despite having created large records management programs, she was apparently seen as a person experienced with filing system but limited as an analyst. What I saw as her wonderful ability to work effectively with all kinds of people did not show up in the oral process as impressively as the self-confident exam-wise smoothness of some of the candidates.

The merit system for civil service has many strengths and virtues, but (as in this case) it is sometimes weak in finding a basis for evaluation which deals with real performance and potential rather than mere examination performance. In keeping supervisors from having too big a role in the process (to avoid personal favoritism and bias), the system can also keep employees from getting appropriate credit for what they have accomplished.

Also, there were some biases which were not removed by the process. For example, women were at a disadvantage in competing for administrative and management positions. Even personnel analysts (mostly male) seemed to share the opinion that women qualified for such positions were (unlike men) rare and exceptional. I was somewhat aware of the problem, probably underestimated its impact, tried quietly to work within the system to help solve it, but ultimately (as in this case) tended to accept it as part of the over-all work environment of the time – one of the things I disliked but could not change. (Was my reaction understandable? Yes. Did I do enough? Probably not. It is easier to adjust to the mistreatment of others if the over-all system is working well for you.)

Anyway, the exam results made it impossible to appoint the person I thought best qualified. Nevertheless the job was filled. I continued my move from heading a management analysis program to assisting the new managers of the department, positioning myself for new opportunities.

As I said at the beginning of this chapter, there is a good deal of difference between directing a program and being an aide to management. In heading a program, there is more of a defined scope, a structure of procedures, a focus on certain objectives. One's identity is bound up in the success of the program. While some support from managers is necessary, a program head can stand a bit apart from management once the program is well established. A program head can identify more with the unit and the program than with the over-all agency and its executives.

As an aide to managers, however, you need to be much less visible and much more committed to what they are trying to do. It helps to keep a low profile, to remain silent about much that you do (because it is supposed to be the work of the manager you are assisting). You have to think as much as possible like your boss, anticipating what the boss would do if doing it personally.

If you draft correspondence, policies, speeches, comments, etc., for a manager to use, you need to be able to write in the style of that manager, rather than your own. (One of the satisfactions of such work is to hear someone say, "I'm sure the Director wrote that, because I recognize his style.")

It is not necessary for an aide and a manager to become close personal friends, but they do need to be able to communicate well with each other. This is a functional inter-relationship, beneficial to both. Sometimes I would disagree with what my boss decided to do, but would provide him with the staff work to help accomplish it. Sometimes, my ideas would be rejected but the effort would still be appreciated.

My personal rule was that if what I was preparing was for someone else to sign, I was obligated to prepare what was wanted. I would also indicate privately to that person my own reaction or suggest some alternative for consideration. On the other hand, I have always felt that what I wrote over my own signature (or signed, regardless of who drafted it) had to reflect my own views, as a matter of personal integrity.

It can get more complicated. I was not always sure whether my bosses were reflecting their own personal ideas or responding to some larger decisions of which I remained largely ignorant. I was uninformed and uninvolved in much of their work. I worked with them only on the things which they chose.

What is the satisfaction of this sort of semi-anonymous staff work? How does it contribute to becoming a manager when it seems so subordinate and passive?

First of all is the satisfaction of competence – of being able to do it well – of being able at least some of the time to do work which a top executive can accept and use as his or her own. Second, one necessarily gets a close-up view of executives at work – warts and all. The boss has to reveal a good deal in order to get good staff assistance. The aide has to think as if in the place of the executive. You can't help but learn to understand executive thinking if you keep trying to put yourself the executive role and preparing material which resembles as much as possible the executive's own.

No doubt, different managers can teach their aides different things. In this case, I worked with at least three very different managers:

1. The Director was the out-front chief executive – always confronted by too much to do and too little time. He could be a harsh critic, but knew what he liked when he saw it and was quick to say so.

2. The political deputy worked much more casually and unpredictably. What he wanted was often merely a sense of the career bureaucrat's slant, or enough of a briefing on technical rules and procedures (which he refused to learn)

to present something in a way a system could accept. In return, he was particularly good at providing colorful and very irreverent personal glimpses of the political players, the game, and his own style of play. To a very interested and appreciative aide, these were real rewards.

3. I remember also some of his personal maxims. Make most phone calls when the other person will not be available. (You want credit for having made the effort, without actually having to talk; the message that you called is enough.) Don't sit through long boring meetings just because people set them up. (Plan ahead to have reasons to skip it, to arrive late, to be called out, to leave early if you decide to.) Don't be trapped into providing an audience for somebody else's show. (You can usually learn more by checking before and after with people who were there.) People who are too busy to attend meetings are usually seen as more important then people who do. (It's like retirement parties: the people who go have to sit and listen to long speeches, while the smart ones send letters which are read aloud from the head table.) Or maybe you just go for the social time (the fun part) and then have to leave.

4. It wasn't that I started doing these things. I just enjoyed hearing his different spin on a world which was clearly not mine. I think I provided something useful in return which every good storyteller needs: a good audience.

5. The administrative deputy was still a different personality: conscientious, careful, and analytical. He gave complete instructions, reviewed what came back very thoroughly, and always expressed thanks for the help. He was the easiest to help, but not necessarily the most fun or the most educational.

There are many ways of assisting managers, many kinds of assignments. Out of those I remember, let me follow one major project to illustrate the process in action: the Governor's Task Force on Reorganization.

A year or so into Governor Brown's new administration, it must have occurred to someone on the Governor's team that it would be timely and useful to launch a study of reorganizing the Executive branch of State Government. The Director of Public Works, my boss, was appointed as a member of a task force which was to make the study and report back to the Governor with recommendations.

This was standard stuff at the time: try to improve efficiency and economy through changes in the structure. Good government. Good politics. A low-risk, low-cost move for which chief executives earned some credit just for trying even if (as often happened) there were few actual results.

In terms of good government, the public administration movement was still somewhat fixed upon the idea of making the Executive branch more of a one-pyramid hierarchy by strengthening the power of the Governor (or any chief executive) over all State administrative agencies. To the extent that such a study produced results, it was predictable that they would involve strengthening the Governor (not, of course, an entirely unattractive proposition to many chief executives).

Governor Brown was already establishing himself as the sponsor of long-range, large-scale plans and projects for California – Higher Education, Water Resources, Highways, etc. To add Reorganization to the list seemed appropriate.

The task force members were chosen both to give some participation on behalf of various interests and to include enough people committed to the Governor's interests to keep the project low-risk. My boss, the Director of Public Works, fit both categories.

The study cost was low (most members served without pay for the honor of it – or for possible benefit to things in which they believed). The staff work was done by people already in State service or working for task force members or both. The members also were well-enough known to the public to merit the standard description: "blue-ribbon panel." If the Governor didn't like the study results he could take credit for having tried, and quietly file the report away.

If he wanted to do some of the things recommended, the report would provide a wonderful basis.

For me, of course, the reorganization project opened up an exciting possibility: participating indirectly, through my boss, in what could be an important effort to improve State administrative organization, the broadest and most comprehensive effort in years.

With one part of my mind I knew that most such studies have little lasting effect. With another part, I hoped that in the particular circumstances (new, action-oriented, liberal administration; continued rapid growth of State government) this study might be an exception. Both personal optimism and professional pragmatism made me willing to set aside doubts, to assume that the study would be important, and to commit myself to helping the Director and the study process in any way I could.

Early on, the task force held an all-day meeting at a nearby University campus to which various officials and experts were invited for a discussion of governmental reorganization. The idea was to gain favorable public attention, to build some preliminary support, and to give an academic base for whatever might come later. Since the invitations to other public officials came from the Governor, it also showed a nice participative spirit on his part. Most of all, it gave the Governor a public pulpit as major speaker of the day.

Like most such speeches, it was put together in his own office by several aides. This one was principally crafted by an aide who had been a long-time attorney and executive in State government, a seasoned bureaucrat respected for political and administrative skills, now a member of the Governor's team, whose special area was liaison between the Governor's office and State agencies (a position usually called Departmental Secretary). He was a member of the reorganization task force and the Governor's principal link with it.

The Departmental Secretary (with the Director's approval) asked me to work with a long-time analyst friend in the Department of Finance and draft some material for the Governor's speech. Once we got over our first reaction (Who, us?) and our second thought (Can we do it?), we set to work with mixed emotions. (What should the Governor say?)

What we came up with (in a very short time – less than a day, I think) was heart-felt, naive and (in retrospect) totally unrealistic. I don't remember most of it, but two points which stick in my mind are enough to give the general idea. First, we wrote a section in which the Governor would pledge himself to support legislation making several partisan elective State offices non-political and appointive (Controller, Secretary of State, Treasurer, Board of Equalization). Second, the Governor would conclude his speech (we proposed) with a clarion call to the citizens of California in general and the forces of good government in particular to join with him and make modernizing State government an immediate and central goal.

What we had done was invent in our own minds a Governor riding on the white horse of good government, ready and eager to do battle for the principles of good organization and civic virtue, unconcerned with politics and practicalities. The Departmental Secretary received the material with friendly thanks and no comments.

A few days later we listened to the Governor's keynote speech at his conference. It was an enlightening experience. He spoke directly to the other elected State officials (most of whom were in the audience). He emphasized their importance in State government. He promised them that he would support the continuation of their elective offices and their independent agencies. Nothing in his reorganization program, he assured them, would have any negative effect on them. In general, the whole tone of the speech was to reassure, to calm fears, to downplay its scope, to portray the study as a modest, safe-and-sane exercise which need not worry the other State political officials.

It was a useful lesson. We had completely misunderstood the situation and misinterpreted the signals we thought had been coming from the Governor, so our proposals (except for a stray word or phrase here and there) were wasted. The Departmental Secretary remained friendly, however, and we continued to do staff work for the task force. I think now that what he was really doing was finding out what a couple of idealistic young career analysts had in mind. We certainly told him. No doubt a very large number of other people were similarly flattered by being asked to submit ideas. As a result the Governor's aides had been able to shape a speech which fit the Governor's objectives while taking into account the attitudes of various interests. It was not a memorable speech, but politically it was an effective one. That it responded to few if any of our hopes was a timely and realistic lesson for us.

With this lesson well in mind, I nevertheless spent the next several months helping the Director in his role as a member of the task force. He asked for a great deal of material and developed his own approach to the project. Working within that approach (and within the Governor's apparent guideline – "don't make waves"), I could nevertheless introduce a few ideas of my own.

I believed that State government had by then reached a size (roughly the scale that the Federal government had reached twenty or thirty years before) in which the major departments needed stronger administration and management capabilities. Instead, the budget, financial, personnel and other administrative services remained highly concentrated, mostly in the Finance Department. Earlier, the Finance department had been innovative in introducing a wide range of new administrative programs and services. By now, it seemed to me, keeping them so highly centralized made the departments too dependent on the Finance department to manage their own affairs well and made the Finance department too large and overloaded with detail to do a good job of over-all executive leadership and planning. A major decentralization of administrative management would make possible better handling of the growth in State government, which was obviously going to continue. I surfaced these ideas when and as I could, but was unable to convince my boss, much less the task force (where the Director of Finance had a powerful influence).

The task force eventually took quite a different course. Instead of favoring decentralization, the task force proposed to move out of the Finance department all but the budget function and the other major controls over State financial administration. The non-financial functions – services such as purchasing, facilities, property management, communications, and parking and automobiles – would go to a new central agency, the General Services department. This plan confirmed the idea that the Director of Finance was overburdened and overextended, but the proposed solution did not decentralize anything. Functions that the Director of Finance considered less important or less necessary for financial control would remain centralized in the new central department.

Decentralization would have been a complex and difficult process, involving rethinking how things should work in both central and operating departments. The task force proposal was, on the other hand, quite easy. The Finance Director and the activities remaining in his department would remain powerful and perhaps become more so. There would be some new executive positions for the Governor and the new department to fill. The activities being moved to the new General Services agency were not in a position to object, even if they were being sent to a less powerful agency (some of the people remaining in the Finance department rather unkindly referred to the people being moved out as the D.O.G.S. – Department of General Services – meaning the "dogs" from the Finance department).

The reorganization plan also had an interesting impact on the Department of Public Works (and on my boss, the Director). The Architecture division was providing a service to State agencies in the design and construction of buildings. It logically belonged in a General Services department. Water Resources had already split off from Public Works to become a separate department, so it could no longer be said that the Public Works department brought together the major State design and construction work. The highways program had become vary large. If the Architecture division were also split off, Public Works would become a highway or transportation agency. My boss did not like the idea of "losing" the Architecture division but did not have an effective alternative to propose.

The real centerpiece of the reorganization proposal was something called the Agency Plan. In traditional reorganization proposals, a major cause of opposition is that in order to create a neater pyramid structure existing agencies are combined into fewer separate units. Naturally the people and agencies affected see this as a "demotion" organizationally. The task force considered many versions of such consolidations, looking for ways to have fewer separate departments reporting directly to the Governor (reducing the Governor's "span of control" as the jargon of the time put it). Eventually, the Departmental Secretary proposed a plan which would leave the existing departments pretty much as they were but add several new executives – Agency Administrators – new positions, each in charge of a group of somewhat related departments. The departments would report to the Governor through one of these new agency heads.

The plan was drawn so that the laws regarding each department were mostly unchanged. The new laws defining the Agency powers were very brief and general. The effect was to arouse relatively little opposition. Some expected the Agency administrator positions to be weak and ineffective, but others saw this weakness as safeguarding existing departments from interference. Some thought that the Agency administrator positions would be strong, and saw this strength as increasing the Governor's role as chief executive. Since it would add quite a number of new high-level political appointees and staff positions, it was attractive to some on those grounds. Others wondered why the Governor could not just have added several Departmental Secretaries to his own staff, but these perhaps underestimated the difference between staff aides and statutory new agency administrators (a new and additional executive level in State government).

On balance, the plan was accepted by the legislature and enacted into law with only a few modifications. Some thought the plan not worth opposing strongly because it did not propose to change things much. Others who might have wanted greater changes could at least be hopeful that the Agency Plan would somehow have a greater impact in time.

What was perhaps less obvious was the importance to the Governor and his administration of adding a significant number of new high-level political executive appointments, people who would serve at the pleasure of the Governor or of his administrators. The activist new administration had found the civil service system unresponsive in some ways. The merit system limited the number of political appointments in each agency to a very few and protected the long-time career service executives against arbitrary dismissal. The Plan added a new group of political appointments in the name of good government and without confronting the civil service system directly.

This study was one of the last of its type in State government. It is ironic that the "principles" of organization which the task force cited as the basis for the Agency plan had already by that time fallen into disfavor in the academic field of public administration. Their validity and appropriateness had been challenged to successfully that they were by now usually referred to, if at all, as "so-called principles." There was skepticism over the value of mere structural reshuffling. Practitioners were becoming more interested in pragmatic approaches focused on group processes and behavior than in redrawing the lines of command.

Task forces have remained a popular device for Governors. In the 1960's, Governor Ronald Reagan appointed a blue-ribbon group from private industry to look for ways to reduce the cost and improve the efficiency of State government. In the 1970's, Governor Jerry Brown (son of Governor Pat Brown) appointed a blue-ribbon task force on reorganization, a much larger group than twenty years before, which in a very different time and style included representatives of many more interests into its membership. Both of these task forces labored for a long time and produced lengthy reports. My impression is that in both the Governor was much less involved personally, and that neither had much lasting impact.

The Agency plan, however, has (with some changes) lasted over the years. Agency Administrators are still a prominent feature of State government. Perhaps there is something to be said for the traditional so-called "principles" of organization if used in a low-risk, low-threat, politically sensitive, pragmatic and sophisticated way. On the other hand, there probably needs also to be – as there apparently was in this case – an underlying set of specific purposes to be accomplished, whether they are revealed at the time or only become apparent later. You usually don't just set out to apply good organization concepts, you use them if they may help you do whatever it is you are trying to do.

Chapter Six

BECOMING A MANAGER

As a *management* analyst, I had learned that I could develop and get approval of changes in administrative organization and management. As a staff assistant to senior managers, both civil service and political types, I could think like a manager, work like a manager, and (it was only a short leap) visualize myself becoming a manager (if I should have the chance).

That chance did come, partly by luck and partly by preparation, the day the political deputy told me that I had been doing a good job, that I had become "part of the team," and that he and the Director would like to promote me when they could. At that point, I said that all they needed to do was set up a second Assistant Director position and appoint me from the current civil service list, on which my name was at the top. (The first Assistant Director position was the one to which the former acting Director of the department had been appointed soon after the new administration had arrived.)

The deputy was, I think, somewhat surprised. He was getting used to the rigid restraints of the civil service system, and probably had not realized how eligible for promotion I had made myself during the interim between administrations. I had decided not to bring it up unless somebody wanted to promote me. In State civil service, it is essential to be on a civil service list, but that alone does not mean a promotion. The person who makes the appointment can choose someone else among the first three interested names on the list or can wait and not appoint anyone until the list expires and a new exam is given.

In any event, the deputy followed through on his words and in a few weeks the Director appointed me to be an Assistant Director, the highest civil service level in the Director's office. It was a major career advancement for me.

In a more personal sense, however, it was really not much of a change. I did many of the same things I had already been doing: acting for the Director and the deputies in administrative matters and assisting them. As a staff aide, I had already been thinking as a manager. I was already trying to handle my work in the way they would have done it if they had the time and interest. As Assistant Director, I still worked this way.

There were, however, two differences: (1) my work was in some respects easier because I would now have some official management authority, and (2) my work would in some respects be harder because I was expected to work with less guidance and with more latitude to make decisions rather than make recommendations.

As an analyst, for example, I had done very little in the Architecture division and focused mostly on the Highways division. More recently, the Architecture division had come under attack and as part of my role in assisting the Director and his deputies, I had been drawn into the issues.

The division was like a large in-house architecture and construction firm, with all State agencies as its "clients" (except for the constitutionally independent University of California). It had the right under civil service to do all this work with its own staff, and contracted work out only when the division decided it could not handle an overload.

Some agencies were critical of the quality of the architectural service and of the buildings it provided. Some of them felt (with reason) that the division was often bureaucratic and unresponsive, that they had too little role as clients in the development and approval of projects, that the process of design and construction was frustratingly slow, and that State buildings were often mediocre in appearance and unfunctional in operation.

Contributing to these negative attitudes was the fact that many design decisions were being made by budget analysts in the Finance department and in the legislative budget office as part of their detailed control of capital outlay projects and costs.

Over the years, Directors of Public Works had kept control of building construction contracting, but otherwise had been much more concerned with the highway program. The Architecture division had accepted having design decisions made by fiscal people because the powerful Finance department could keep dissatisfied client agencies under control. The result was the State buildings were designed to look inexpensive and plain. The fiscal reviews tended to focus on appearance (ceiling heights, surface materials, decoration and ornament, space allocations – anything which might add to cost but not be essential). Many architects on the staff had become weary of defending designs against budget critiques and felt it was better to go along and get along. The budget analysts had the sincere conviction that they were reducing costs and avoiding waste, as their bosses expected.

Meanwhile, with a new administration in Sacramento and a growing State building program under way, the California organization of professional architects looked at these projects and saw millions in architectural work which was outside their reach. It was not difficult for them to conclude that it would be a public service for them to get the rules changed to allow the State to contract with private architectural firms rather than have the work done by a civil service architectural office. (There was no particular controversy over the construction contracting or the earthquake safety review of local plans which the division also handled.) Civil service architects in the division had not been active in professional organizations of architects, even in Sacramento. When the dividing lines were drawn, the public architects were regarded as "they" (civil servants) rather than "we" (architects) by most members of the profession.

When I began to act for the Director and the deputies in approving and awarding construction contracts, it included building projects. However, this did not require me to pay much attention to the architectural aspects. Under the State Contract Act, as interpreted by the department's attorneys, it was a matter of seeing that the required form and procedures had been followed rather than a matter of reviewing the project as a whole.

This was a bit ironic. Personally, I had for a long time had a lay interest in architecture and particularly in contemporary design from the Bauhaus school on. My wife and I had long sought out what we felt were the best modern designs within our means, in furniture, in other household items, in houses. Eventually, we had an architect-designed contemporary house built for us in Sacramento. All this, however, was entirely personal and separate from my State work (except that I did learn as a client how frustrating, expensive, irritating, and difficult it can be to turn the exciting theories of modern architectural design into practical built reality).

When the architectural controversies began to boil up, it touched in me another more work-related belief – that public service could and should be of the highest quality, and should be protected from narrow or selfish interests. I felt that:

1. the State's architectural work needed improvement,

2. the problems went beyond the public architects to the whole system in which they worked,

3. given an opportunity and incentives to improve, public architects could in time do as good work as private architects,

4. some reasonable combination of in-house and contract design would probably work best, and

5. the division should be protected from unfair attacks and from efforts to divert its work to private interests while it undertook the necessary improvements.

At about this time, a Master Plan for higher education in California had been completed. It was a successful and widely accepted study, the basis for many changes. One aspect was to take the State colleges out of the Department of Education (and away from their historic roots as teachers colleges). The goal was for State colleges to become a separate and parallel university system, with a governing board and independence more like the University of California. The legislation to implement this part of the Master Plan provided that, like the University of California, the new State Universities and Colleges system could handle its own architectural and building construction as it chose, without regard to civil service restrictions.

About half the workload of the Architecture division was suddenly at stake, The Public Works department, not involved in higher education planning, had been slow to become aware of these developments and slower to assess the seriousness of their impact. The Governor supported the Master Plan. The State colleges were determined to break the monopoly the Architecture division had enjoyed and to emulate the University of California. The Finance department's budgetary control was not being challenged, so it was not opposed. The administration was unlikely to defend a civil service system it generally considered too restrictive. The organization of state employees would automatically oppose the change, as a matter of principle, but otherwise there would be few allies on this issue.

At this point, still an analyst and not yet a manager, I took a somewhat quixotic initiative. It seemed to me that the department was too focused on highway matters to give this matter the attention it urgently needed. I felt that I had the background, interest, and perspective to see the whole issue and I wanted to work on it. I thought it might be possible to develop a plan which would meet the needs of all concerned while giving the Architecture division time in which to respond to the new situation.

Without saying anything or asking permission, I simply gave myself an assignment to prepare a proposal for the Director suggesting both a general strategy and specific tactics. It was a lengthy memo – perhaps a dozen pages – but much more personal and punchy than my usual analyst style. It read more like a proposal to a colleague, taking for granted what we both already knew and leaving the assumptions largely unstated and presenting many suggestions in as few words as possible, in checklist form so they could be accepted or not, one by one.

The underlying strategy was, on the one hand, to accept the proposed new authority for the new State university system over its architectural and construction services, and on the other hand, to extend as long as possible the time in which the Architecture division would continue to handle most or all of the work. (The new State university governing board and their new staff would have a huge number of pressing things to do at the start, so they might see the practical wisdom of continuing to use our services for a while.)

This interim would allow several things to happen. First, there would be a major marketing of the present strengths and successes (there were some – such as the handling of construction contracts and the supervision of private construction contractors). Some of the recent designs (not necessarily for colleges) were in fact rather handsome, and even ordinary buildings look better in color; we needed a book of striking photographs by talented photographers. The pictures would also implicitly show the exceptional variety and range of the division's work.

We also needed to have careful and direct cost comparisons of similar buildings done by the division for colleges and by contract architects for the University of California campuses. With rapid growth, both appearance and cost were important. The presentation of costs in an easily understood form would help discourage simplistic or sweeping over-generalizations. The audiences for this material would be the leaders of the new organization. It was time to treat clients as clients. (It would also be useful with the Governor and other key State executives and legislators and their staffs.)

Second, we would emphasize the large and difficult burden, the complexity, the administrative detail which the division had been handling for the college system. It would be useful for them to understand the organization and staff they would need to develop to take over this work, and at the same time to reassure them that the division was willing to continue to handle it while they dealt initially with more urgent matters. The timing of the change-over would be up to them. (Given the State's pace of building project design and construction, acceptance of this approach would probably allow the division several years in which to continue most services).

Third, and most important, the division must set out immediately to improve the quality of its work, its presentations, and its relationships with college system clients. It would be clear that the future of the division and its employees depended on becoming as entrepreneurial, as service-minded, as competent and as efficient as major private firms. If successful, the division could continue to do a major portion of the college work indefinitely. The new situation could be used to release talented architects on the staff from frustrating and inappropriate controls, since the fiscal analysts could hardly impose tighter controls on in-house architects than on the private contract architects doing similar projects. Also, the division was experienced in handling many projects where engineering or modifications of existing structures were involved.

It was this initiative – this memo, this strategic proposal – which caused the deputy to say I had made myself part of the team. Many of the ideas became part of the Director's plans (along with other ideas as well). I took on a major responsibility for continuing to monitor and manage the department's interests in this policy area, and in the process worked much more informally and independently under their general guidance.

What happened to the division? The strategy worked well and did gain needed time in which to improve. The new system decided to have all construction contracting and supervision handled by the division indefinitely. All current projects already in the division for design were left there. For several years at least, the division was assured of at least half of all the new building projects of the new system. At several new and existing campuses, the division was chosen as the campus architect, for campus planning and coordination of projects handled by both public and contract architects. Some of the best division architects became active in the professional organizations, which helped to bridge the gap between public and private practice. Some private architects (mostly the larger firms) had a new opportunity to do more State work under a more flexible system. Perhaps the new competition helped stimulate better design from all concerned. The staff architects with the most talent and commitment in the division seemed to thrive in response to the new challenges and opportunities.

Looking back, it seems to me that this was when I really became a manager – when I moved from working primarily with the ways and means of administration to taking the lead in relation to a broad public policy issue. The change was a matter of degree, not a difference of kind. The problem was more complicated, the factors were more varied, the decisions left to me were greater, and so was my personal involvement and commitment. I had done everything before to some extent, but not this much or all at once. There was another more personal difference. As an analyst or an aide, I could handle much of the work in a sort of technical skilled way, applying what I had learned to do to what I had been assigned to do. When I finally spoke up and took the initiative on the architecture problem, it was because I felt deeply and personally about it and because I had confidence in my ability to be a leader in developing a solution.

The outcome was both good administration and good politics. Everybody won; nobody was defeated. The public interest was served.

PART TWO

MANAGER IN ACTION

Snapshot (1960)

WHEN I THINK of myself at forty-one, I picture a family. I was no longer a young beginner, starting out on my own, but a mid-career manager, a husband, and a father of three. The times were different, too. It was no longer the early post-World War II period of newly-won peace and hope but the full-fledged Cold War period of endless global conflict and hidden fears – a strange time of mixed feelings, somewhere between optimism and apocalypse.

What did I look like by then? I was still young-looking enough to be called "young man" or (even more irritating) "son" by some more senior and perhaps less secure managers. I was not one to offer a respectful "Sir" in return.

I cultivated the Oppenheimer look (crew-cut hair), the executive look (dark-rim plastic glasses, a different suit for each day of the week, restrained ties), the fortysomething look (serious manner, slightly stressed and always busy). Inside, I felt much more self-confident (perhaps a bit too much so) after a string of very good years.

My personal goals and values had not changed much, but by this time I was more pragmatic and flexible about the ways and means of achieving them. I was as strongly committed as ever to the value of public service and the ideals of good government. I still believed in the power of rational analysis and problem-solving to bring about progressive changes. However, by this time I also thought of myself as a fairly seasoned bureaucrat who understood how State government worked and could get things done by applying that knowledge (these two are not incompatible, but they are also not quite the same thing).

I was as committed to marriage, home and family and enjoyment of the California good life as to my profession as a public manager. Basically the two were integrated, but sometimes the daily demands of personal and family and work life were very stressful. I was working very hard, but it was the close partnership with my wife which made it possible to keep everything in balance. (Some of the stress must have shown: one year my son gave me for my birthday a toy figure of a man bent over carrying a heavy sack on his back – "because you work so hard," he said.)

It amuses me now to hear some people poke fun at the early TV show "Father Knows Best" as the essence of 1950s unreality. the impossibly, stereotypically "happy" family – wise father, loving mother, capable older daughter, inquiring son, clear-eyed younger daughter, spacious house, serious family discussions, always-solvable problems, the feeling of optimism and togetherness. Yes, of course we recognized at the time how simplified, exaggerated, even cartoonish it was. After all, it was a TV sitcom – but it was funny, touching and appealing, a hopeful version to us of our family in a few years. Unrealistic? Then life should become more like TV.

All the dark worries and disappointments of the post-war era were still there, but buried deep. After a while, when threats are endless and seem totally out of your control, you try to put them out of your mind. We knew all about the atom bomb and the apocalypse that waited only for the touch of a button by somebody somewhere. We all knew the unthinkable cost and the draining social impact of the atomic arms race. So we accepted that all those threats were part of our world, but tried to build a good life for ourselves and our children anyway.

Perhaps we excluded too much, accepted too much of the world as it was. There were a lot of other serious problems besides the Cold War which were set aside until later.

Perhaps we expected too much, hopeful that as time passed things would somehow just get better. Perhaps we had too much confidence in our own generation, expecting that it would soon lead the world in a new and better direction. (When John F. Kennedy was elected President, that hopeful era of new leadership seemed at hand.)

Perhaps we passed along to our children not only the values of education and idealism and affluence, as we intended, but some of the deeper and mostly unspoken feelings of disappointment and impending doom, as well.

I remember that at about this time (1960), my father (stroke-ravaged and bed-ridden in a Southern California nursing home, but clear-headed and with plenty of time to think) startled me by remarking that he had lived in much better times than I would experience. His generation, he said, had enjoyed a wonderful era of progress, but now he felt some sort of turning point had been reached. From here on, he said, things would get worse. He added that he was glad not to have to live through it. He died later that year.

At the time, I thought it was just his time of life and his situation. Everything was going so well for me. Why wouldn't it continue, if I kept on managing well? To me, the future looked bright. Looking back now, I wonder if he was feeling something much more basic.

Capter Seven

DAY BY DAY

MANAGEMENT INVOLVES MAJOR policies and projects, but daily routines usually take up most of a manager's time. The ultimate success of a manager may depend on how a limited number of important matters are handled, but how the daily routines and details are handled may also make a considerable difference – especially, the extent to which the manager is able to use the details to help accomplish larger purposes.

Fair enough. But how does one know what is important? Here sits the manager at a desk, typically a desk with some sort of baskets or folders for papers (In, Out, Hold, Read, Action, or some such organizing categories), plus telephones, visitor chairs, a meeting table, and (these days) probably a computer and a fax machine.

Why is it likely to be set up this way? Because the manager is connected to various communication systems and work procedures which (among other things) bring information and work in and out. Some of these have been set up by others or are firmly established in the organization. To these a manager will largely adjust. Others are more personal choices which fit the way the manager prefers to work. The combination tends to set the style and pace of daily routines.

What is routine? Basically, anything a manager does which is predictable and repetitive and has only a short-term impact. For these, pre-set systems can be developed: if this happens, do this; when you want this result, do this; when you do this, do it this way. The question is not whether the matter is important or not (some routine matters are very important to somebody), but whether it can be handled largely by methods established in advance and whether it is appropriate to do so.

These are, of course, judgments. Usually, some process has at least partially sorted out the apparently routine matters from the exceptional and has put them into the manager's work flow. The manager needs to make some quick choices – on the one hand, do

I need to handle this personally; if so, what kind of attention does it need; if not, where should it go, and for what purpose?

The usual managerial rule is to do personally as little routine work as possible – a sort of appropriate laziness. If you handle it personally, it should be because this is in some way necessary. If someone else can handle it, fine. The choice, however, is not merely a matter of yes or no. There are other considerations.

For example, take a simple matter: a letter needs to be answered. Even if you don't need to prepare the reply, there may be other questions. Is a written reply best? Does it need to be acknowledged first? Is it from a source to whom we should be particularly sensitive? Are there any long-term effects? What should we be trying to accomplish? To avoid? Has there been related correspondence? Who should sign the reply? Who needs to clear the reply before it goes out (often, several people)? Any guidance or comments needed? Do you want to see the reply? Before or after it goes out? Who needs copies, inside and outside, of the letter, the reply, or both? These are routine questions.

At a different level, different questions. How many of these choices can be set up ahead of time as a process to be handled by others? Is it worth developing pattern paragraphs or sample replies for frequent use? What safeguards do you want on the system? How can you make it flexible enough that exceptional cases will still get special handling? Who can intervene to override the system when necessary?

The key is to manage the routine flow, rather than focus on each individual item as if it were unique – whether it be letters, phone calls, visitors, faxes, meetings, or other types of communications. You need to look for ways to turn routine actions into appropriate systems (when it is worth the time and effort to do so). You need to manage the "in basket" of incoming communications, not be managed by it; otherwise you can be overwhelmed with details and trapped into unwanted ways of working.

Even when you see the need to systematize day-by-day routines, you may not need to develop the systems yourself. If other people can develop the systems for you, fine. If other people can supervise for you the people who develop the systems, even better. Just make sure you are still the manager. As manager, you need to see that (1) others involved have the information and training they need, (2) the systems provide for exceptions and unexpected issues to be spotted and dealt with in a non-routine way, and (3) you personally still know what you need in order to perform your role.

A second type of routine managerial work is "keeping in touch." These are the things which don't require action, but which you may need to know simply as part of the environment of your job. Managers live and work on the basis of information, they hunger for it, they need to "know the territory." However, so much information is available (especially these days) that just "keeping informed" would often be far more than a full-time job. Somewhere in that haystack of information may be just the needle you urgently need – but you can't spend all your time looking for it.

As with routine action systems, the key is to manage the flow. Many action items are also useful as information – the two overlap. Some information you will know in advance that you need. Some can come as regular reports. Some can be scanned or screened by others on whatever basis you jointly develop. Others may be on a "when-and-if" basis – information wanted only when you ask or only when certain things happen or at certain points in a process or in preparation for certain events.

Once you start thinking along these lines, common sense takes you a long way. Fortunately, there are a great many ways to get and to give information. Remember also that you are also a source of information for others, and these outward flows should also be a part of the systems.

Unfortunately, some managers see only their need to receive information and pay little attention to the needs of others. Those who see information as part of their power base may actively seek to withhold information or to limit access by subordinates and peers. In fairness, it should be said that this same tactic is also used by some subordinates to block information flow to their bosses and higher management. The usual method is to require that the information flow along command channels, so it can be controlled and restricted and delayed (usually in the name of "being sure it is correct" or of "interpreting" it or "being helpful"). It is well known, of course, that "outside" access to information is also managed (i.e. controlled and restricted) in many organizations. This has in fact become a large and important type of specialized staff work.

So far as management theory is concerned, there is no "principle" which says that information should flow along the lines of command, either up or down the hierarchy. The line of command need not be the information channel. In fact, it would usually be quite impossible to operate completely in this way. Common sense indicates that routine information often needs to flow as directly and promptly as possible from sources to users. There may often be a need to provide additional information, as well – to explain, to comment, to summarize, to interpret – but that need does not usually justify blocking or delaying the basic routine flow.

It seems to me that these days the management information problem should be turned upside-down. The first managerial concern should be to see that others, from the grass-roots up, have a flow of routine information which enables them to work to their full capacity.

We have the technology now to provide user-controlled information networks and flows. Instead of restricting information flow on the basis of rank and hierarchy, centralizing and limiting access, we need to encourage people to seek what they need to know and use. Management would still have its special information needs, as do all other parts of an organization, but managers would not have the burden of planning and deciding for the whole organization who can know what and why.

A third kind of routine management activity is to keep in touch with reality. As you put more routines on "automatic pilot," are you still flying the plane? How would you know when to resume control? The systems should include some safeguards of this type, but you also need early warnings from outside the systems – and, if possible, from more than one source.

One simple safeguard is known as "management by walking around." It is a smart idea, no matter how good the flow of information, to get up and out of your office, to look around, to get around, to go places you don't have to go, to talk with people you don't usually see. You will find that you pick up all sorts of impressions and clues and hunches about what is happening. It is also much easier for people to say things to you in a casual contact, if they want to, and to let you know things they would never come to your office to report (no matter how "open" you say your office door is).

"Walking around" also has symbolic value. It says what kind of a person you are (or want to be). The manager who only goes to the offices of superiors and peers and has everyone else come to her (or his) office is probably missing a lot of useful information (and useful exercise, as well).

All this may work to conserve your time and energy, but as you work to turn daily details into routine systems, remember that other people are playing the same game. People in organizations constantly make work for each other. Your staff, your peers, your bosses, the administrative service units, the operating units – all will, like you, probably be busily devising routine procedures which help them but which are likely to require of you some of that time you are saving.

What can you do in self-defense? One approach is to try to "read" the incoming information and the demands for your personal attention, in order to assess their real importance (as distinct from their official or apparent status). So much is done in organizations "in the name of" the managers, especially the chief executive. It becomes difficult to separate out what they really, personally are involved with and what (much the larger part) they are really just signing or passing along without much personal concern.

Organizations use symbols – titles, letterheads, signatures, etc. – to signal status and importance. The symbols say, "Important person. Pay attention to this message." But in large organizations, there are too many messages from authoritative sources. You can't take them all as being equally important. So you look for clues.

What do you look for? Here are some examples. Does this message seem consistent with what else you know about the apparent source? Does it seem the manager wrote it personally, or merely signed someone else's draft? Is it really intended for you personally (no matter how it is addressed), or is it enough that you just note and pass along? Is it worth asking a question or two, or having an aide do a little scouting in order to get a better feel for the situation? How are other managers reacting? What does your staff suggest?

In some organizations, a different set of clues are used on the paradoxical basis that the personal is more important that the merely official. When too many official messages may cause them all to seem routine, apparent personal touches are added to show importance: writing in the first name of the addressee; signing with a first name only; adding a brief handwritten personal note; making a follow-up contact (or having it made by an aide); bringing the matter up at a meeting. These clues may be important matters of organizational etiquette or merely amusing personal tactics, depending on the organization.

The more general point is that managers often spend a good deal of time thinking about the style of doing something, not just the substance. Consciously or not, managers develop a personal style: offhand, casual and friendly; formal, official and remote; somewhat the same with all; varied according to the situation or mood or audience, etc. It is a matter both of what works and what fits the manager.

Many managers prefer a style which is concise but low key, emphasizing requests rather than authority. The really powerful executive rarely needs to emphasize authority directly; quiet suggestions and a degree of informality can communicate it well enough. The symbols of office and the attitudes of aides often magnify the power and status of the boss; in person the manager can rely on this impressive context (without seeming to be aware of it), and underplay the role to good effect.

Despite all these tactics for time-saving routines, most managers complain to some degree of an overload of information and a lack of time. It is not uncommon for a manager's entire style and daily routines to be built on the assumption that speeding through the daily calendar is the highest priority of all. It is often pointed out, in support of such a pace, that even the hardest working executive has only a limited number of hours in which to get things done.

While I have certainly lived (unhappily) through too many overcrowded work days, I think that nevertheless the emphasis on "time management" may focus too much on the wrong problem and the wrong solution.

I believe that many managers are uncomfortable and even apprehensive if they are not busily in action every moment. Performing little visible physical "work," they want always to be loaded with appointments, meetings, phone calls, travel, etc. – most of which tend to deal with current and near-term events.

Since managers live on being able to read their organizations and situations, they also become uncomfortable and even apprehensive if they don't feel they know enough about what is happening. Like news-junkies, some managers hunger for the latest word – whether they need to know or not. (The myth of the all-seeing, all-knowing, all-wise manager can have a bad effect.)

Managers tend to learn their ways of working by imitating other managers – either from experience or from popular images or both. In this way, they sometimes pick up, internalize and turn into habits ways of working which have not been carefully thought through. Habits of self-management are particularly likely to escape critical scrutiny. After all, if you have been successful enough to get where you are, it is easy to feel you must be doing things right. Managers who are skilled in critically evaluating others may find self-evaluation too sensitive a task.

There is a tendency to assume that adding more people to help will ease the manager's workload. In fact, it may well increase it. The help of aides comes with some degree of added burden for the manager – just relating to them and maintaining a situation in which aides can be effective takes some time and effort.

Some aides tend to relate their own importance to the amount of attention they get from superiors. Others are adept at passing upward a flow of problems which keep the manager busy with staff-initiated assignments.

Bosses, too, can be problems if they work (as some do) on the assumption that all their concerns are automatically of first priority for their subordinates. Such a manager can preempt large chunks of time. Specialists in organizations also have their ways of helping to overwhelm managers with detail and jargon.

The result of such factors, often working in deadly combination, is (1) overload, or (2) capture by staff, or (3) frustration – too much to do (or to do well) within available time and attention.

"Captured" means a manager who becomes a mere signature machine or automatic approval point, relying on others so much that personal decisions are rare and abilities atrophy. Such a person remains a manager in title and on the chart, but in reality leaves most decisions to others.

Frustration often comes with the sense of "Why can't I get anything done around here?" Even effective managers need patience with long lead-times, complex processes, and uncontrollable outcomes. Some frustration is normal, but at a point it can become overwhelming.

I believe some managers react to overload, ineffectiveness and frustration with an excessive focus on personal survival and personal benefits. Those who seek all manner of personal status and rewards at the expense of the organization are often interpreted as greedy, selfish, or manipulative. In some cases, at least, it may be a kind of abdication from the complexities of leadership to a simpler self-centered role.

All of the above factors lead to the conclusion that how routine day-by-day management is handled is an important aspect of managing. If too much daily detail floods in, it inhibits necessary thinking, planning, and initiative. If too much is diverted to others, the manager risks becoming ineffective.

One needs to balance and adjust the handling of "routine" matters, so that it continues to fit shifting priorities and situations. What is "right" at one time is "wrong" at another. What is "routine" now may be "non-routine" later. In normal times, the adjustments can be made slowly. In a crisis, everything else may suddenly be set aside for the time being as "routine."

It all depends on what you (and others) are trying to do, the situations in which you are working, and the choices available to you. In any event, how routine matters are handled is too important to be handled in a routine way.

Chapter Eight

POLITICS

PUBLIC ADMINISTRATION THEORY tries to reconcile two very different ideas: political leaders (for democratic responsiveness to the public) and professional managers (for administrative efficiency and economy). At first, it was thought that there should be a clear line separating the two. When it was obvious that the line was not (and could not be) clear, the idea became that the two should interact but with the professional executives always responsive to the political leaders.

As a professional manager in State government, I worked directly for political executives. They were appointed by the Governor (or by Governor-appointed officials). I had been appointed through the career civil service system. Having reached our positions by two such different routes, we found ourselves working closely together, with much in common but with some very different loyalties and concerns as well.

In this situation, the interaction was not an abstract theory but a personal daily reality. I want to talk about this in personal and practical terms – not to contribute to theory but as a personal experience. I do feel that this relationship of politics and administration is a crucial and distinctive area of public management.

When I first started working with political appointees, as a management analyst, the ground rules seemed quite clear. I was an in-house consultant, working on assignments mostly initiated by political executives, who were the clients for my services. Clearly, the authority was entirely with the clients. My only influence was the persuasiveness of my reports, the power of my research, and the professional integrity of my work.

It was more or less assumed (for purposes of the studies) that we had a common interest in good administration, and that there was no conflict between good administration and good politics. The studies were mostly of internal ways and means, not of public policies. In any event, the climate of the time was such that political executives generally respected and encouraged the independent integrity of applied administrative research. They might well reject or ignore the results, but they seldom intervened in the process.

When I became a manager in a large department, I was still working as a career professional. In many ways there was still no conflict between good administration and good politics. In some ways, however, the interaction became more complex.

- Less separation. There was no longer a different process to distinguish what I was doing as a career manager and what the political managers were doing. Some of the work might be done by one or the other, or (more often) by both working together.

- Broader issues. The subjects now could involve interests of the current political administration. For example, the issue of architectural services was both a political and an administrative issue. In working with the issue, I became a member of a team led by political executives.

- More interaction. In order to work together so closely, a good deal of information needed to be exchanged. I needed to understand the evolving political goals in order to help put them into action. Political executives needed to know what I was doing and what I was learning in the process. If the interaction worked well, the initial caution gradually changed to mutual trust.

- Mutual accommodation. Career and political people do not have the same agenda. Political goals are to (1) stay in office, and (2) carry out political programs. Career goals are to (1) respond to political leadership, (2) provide public services, and (3) protect the non-political merit system. Both need to work with the common areas and respect the differences. The career group should not be used in ways which impair its ability to serve the next political group which comes to office. The career group should not obstruct or undermine the political leadership. There is, however, a responsibility to both executive and legislative political

> officials and, beyond that, to the laws rather than the leaders.

For a long time, the political-career relationship in State service did not seem difficult. The changes from one moderate Republican administration to another seemed more a matter of new people coming in than of new policies.

The change from Republican to Democratic administration was a more definite break. There was a much longer period of personal and political adjustments before the political-career gap began to close. The differences in policies, partisanship and style were much greater. It seemed to me, however, that the transition still worked reasonably well.

In some cases, career managers with long tenure had developed strong ties of mutual interest with legislators and with interest groups. They looked not so much to the Governor as to other sources for guidance. Not all political appointees were experienced in leading large organizations. While some were outstanding managers, others were chosen for other reasons. When confronted with a gap between their official authority and their ability to get things done, it was easy to blame the bureaucrats for being unresponsive and obstructionist. When citizens and taxpayers complained, when anger and frustration rose, it was easy in complex situations to pass the blame on from politicians to bureaucrats.

I had no personal problem with the new leadership of my department. In fact, the new situation was very good for me. I was surprised when the Democratic administration eventually targeted for attack the civil service system and more specifically the appointment and tenure of career civil service managers.

It was called the Career Executive plan. It was based on a simple set of ideas: (1) State career managers are not responsive enough to political managers; (2) the reason is that they are too protected by civil service appointments and tenure; (3) if career managers could more easily be demoted or replaced, they (and the rest of the civil service) would become more responsive to political leadership, and (4) better and more democratically responsible State government would result.

There were, however, some safeguards for civil servants in the plan, which I believe had been negotiated with the managers of civil service system by the administration: (1) those already in career executive civil service positions would not be affected; (2) demoted managers could return to their previous lower-rank civil service positions; (3) competition for career executive positions would in future be limited to those already in State civil service; and (4) political managers would be able to appoint career executives from a larger number of people on the list than in "regular" civil service.

The plan was introduced by the Governor and his administration as an important and progressive reform. It was supported by the central personnel agency which operated the civil service system. Word was passed to State employees, "Don't oppose this or you will get something you will like even less." Those already in career manager positions were reassured that it would not affect them personally. Those who hoped to become State career managers could feel that eliminating outside competition for such appointments might offset the reduced job security – and anyway you could still return to your old job, if demoted.

To me, the whole scheme amounted to nothing more than a clever attempt to weaken and intimidate career managers. It was a political attack on the merit system. I felt duty-bound to make clear what I felt were unfair and damaging aspects of the proposal.

I was no Don Quixote. I had no illusions that I could block the outcome. Most civil service leaders had already given their support to what they had decided was the best compromise under the circumstances. Most civil service employees had decided (1) "It doesn't affect me much personally," or (2) "What I think won't make any difference anyway," or (3) "I don't want to get involved" because (a) it's already a done deal, or (b) to do so might hurt my career, or (c) it could be worse, or (d) some combination of the above.

I, on the other hand, felt that I had to speak out in some way because I felt deeply and personally about the issue. At the same time, however, I was sensible enough to want a way to do so which would reduce risks of reprisal or career damage.

As I was pondering what to do and how to do it, I received an unexpected invitation from the Sacramento chapter of the American Society for Public Administration, a professional society of government administrators and teachers. The Career Executive Plan was to be the topic of a debate at the next meeting. The head of the State personnel agency had agreed to present the Pro side, but they were having trouble (the program arranger said) in getting someone to present the Con side. Would I be willing to do it? It was an ideal forum – a conspicuous, well-attended meeting, a professional non-political setting, and an equal debate with an important official. I accepted at once.

The Career Executive Plan, I felt, rested on two wrong assumptions: first, that career managers often improperly resist and are unresponsive to political officials because they have job security; and, second, that limiting competition for such positions to people already in State service is a necessary safeguard against a political influx.

The case which I made against the plan in debate was fairly direct.

1. Career executives need to be selected and evaluated through rigorous but non-political processes.

2. Career executives, like all civil servants, are responsible to political officials, but not exclusively to them. They are also responsible for carrying out the laws, for providing professional advice, and for maintaining the integrity of the public service. The political relationship therefore sometimes involves stress and conflict.

3. Political officials do not need and should not have the power of arbitrarily removing and demoting career executives. Under such pressure career executives will show less initiative and take less responsibility.

4. The concept of closed promotions (which the career executive proposal extended) is not a necessary or appropriate part of a merit system. The merit principle means competition at all levels, open to qualified applicants both inside and outside State service.

I argued that career managers are generally eager to respond to political leaders – almost too much so, in some cases. The power of political officials over subordinates is already very great and does not need to be increased.

To me, the plan reduced protection against arbitrary political abuse in exchange for increased protection against outside competition – an improper political advantage in exchange for an improper employee advantage, a bad bargain both ways. The concepts of merit competition, professional public service and good government would suffer.

If reform is needed, I suggested that it should focus on the opposite for career managers: open the entry gates wider to increase open competition, but continue to protect managers against political abuse. Also, testing and evaluation procedures should be reviewed to make them as realistic and valid as possible.

I believed that if the Career Executive Plan was enacted, it would be a first step toward weakening and demoralizing the strong civil service system in California State government. It would be a declaration that career managers were regarded as problems, not professionals – that they needed the threat of arbitrary partisan political power to make them behave responsibly.

In time, it seemed likely that the State service would develop cadres of career executives – some loyal to one political group, some to another – each rising or falling according to political changes, rather than by merit. Or they would simply become passive and demoralized in the face of political power and distrust, keeping their heads down and trying to keep out of trouble by playing it too safe. I expected that more career managers would leave, and that some potential talent would be lost from State service.

The debate at the meeting went well, from my point of view. I made my points with the strong conviction which I felt, and that seemed to reach the audience of State employees and officials positively. The Pro side was presented very well, but with perhaps a more detached, analytical tone. (Odd that I, the analyst, should have turned advocate so strongly on this occasion.)

After the debate, I received many favorable comments – at least, I took the general tone of "I admire your guts" to be favorable. I wrote out my remarks, sent copies to those who asked, and otherwise closed down the subject entirely. I had gone about as far as I felt I could go, in this situation. I did not want to become a martyr. A few months later, as expected, the Career Executive Plan became law.

I have never changed my opinion on this subject. I believe that this partisan plan did start a downward spiral in the situation of career managers and eventually of other civil service employees in State government. Some thought the plan was a compromise which would protect civil service from further attacks, but it did not accomplish this. I felt better for having publicly had my say.

Interesting footnote: a few months after all this, I was appointed by the Governor to a political deputy position. It defied the conventional wisdom for a civil servant to oppose the administration openly (even if carefully) on a political issue and be rewarded with political advancement. Maybe it showed that my fears of political power were exaggerated. Maybe it just made people notice me in a different way. Maybe there was no connection at all.

In any event, I crossed the line from civil service to political service. The conventional wisdom on this kind of move was that it was a one-way trip: you can never go back to where you were. A friend who had been there and back put it to me this way, "You have a right to return to your civil service job, but people will know you have been political and they won't stop seeing you that way. You won't be a virgin anymore, and you can't get your virginity back. So think carefully before you make the move."

What brought about my political appointment was a curious combination of events plus a little initiative on my part. The Governor's reorganization plan took the Architecture division out of the Public Works department and moved it into a new General Services department, along with other central administrative services and facilities which had been in the Finance department. The plan was to turn the Public Works department into a sort of Transportation department, responding to the frequent criticism that highways (and not other forms of transportation) received most of the State's attention and most of the transportation money.

Meanwhile, the Agency Plan (the keystone of the reorganization) was to add a layer of new Agencies (and Agency Administrators) between the Governor and the existing Directors (and departments).

My boss, the Public Works director, was to become Administrator of the Transportation and Business Agency. Somebody new would become Public Works director. The Administrator would bring along into the new office his political deputy, some secretaries and aides, and me, a career manager. I took on the assignment of seeing that space was remodeled for the new Agency. It needed to be ready by January 1, when the reorganization law would take effect.

It all seemed to be going smoothly according to plan when suddenly, a few weeks before the move, the political deputy told me that the layout for the new Agency office (which he seemed to have forgotten he had once approved) did not provide him with a workable office. He said that he would have to occupy instead the office which I had thought was to be for me, which left me no place. It was an indirect but unmistakable way of telling me that I was not going to be a part of the new Agency team, but would stay where I was as Assistant Director of Public Works.

I did not object, did not even question. The decision had been made. I had no "right" to the new position. I did ask the deputy whether I could move into his old Public Works office when he left (a handsome well-located space). I figured he owed me that much.

After that, I could have stayed on as Assistant Director while the new Director arrived, the department became a highways-only agency (with a little transportation planning on the side), and the department-agency adjustments were worked out. There might be some risks for me in the changes, but they would probably have been manageable.

On the other hand, I was personally more and more in sympathy with the increasing criticisms of the highway program: its one-dimensional focus on more and more freeways; its arbitrary ramming of routes through cities; its lack of concern for negative environmental effects on air quality and the environment. The highway-building machine, designed to engineer and build highways with a generous supply of Federal and State gas tax money, seemed to be turning into a sort of juggernaut on automatic pilot as it cut its freeway networks through the cities. Many groups were trying to change the planning process and the values by which transportation decisions were made.

In one sense, all that was not really my business. I dealt with construction contracts, administration and other ways and means. I could just focus on them and on the very competent engineers with whom I worked. However, I have always worked better when I am enthusiastic about the programs and convinced of their benefits. So I looked around for possible alternatives to just staying on – and soon found a good possibility.

The new General Services department, to which the Architecture division would soon move, would have some new managers – a Director and two deputies, all political appointments. I thought there might be a place there for me.

I had become deeply involved in the administration of the Architecture division in helping it hang on to the State universities and colleges as a client, and to improve the quality of its architectural services. I enjoyed architecture as a personal interest more than I did highway engineering. By now a new State Architect was heading the division, bringing new talent and ideas. Both its architectural design and its relations with its clients were showing definite improvement.

I was also involved with the Architecture division in another way: as Assistant Director, I was handling approval of the construction contracts for State buildings – which at the time amounted, as I recall, to about $100 million.

When the reorganization legislation was being drafted, I urged that the effective date be moved off until July 1, to provide more time for the new department to become ready to handle to handle this contracting responsibility. The staff, however, was under orders that the date had to be January 1 (only a short time away). It was obviously going to be a concern for the new department that there be no breakdown in the contracting process and that authority over contracting be maintained, especially at the start.

Here I am, I thought, with a specific management skill which not very many people have, and there, I thought, is a new department which will urgently need someone with that skill. It seemed to me that I might become a deputy director in the new department, if I played my cards right. I decided to get into the game.

How do you get appointed by the Governor to a political position when you are not seen as political? Here is the way it worked for me.

1. The real appointment selection would be made by the Director of Finance (with, of course, the Governor's approval). He was anxious to get rid of a lot of functions which would go to the new department. He wanted to concentrate on budget and finance and on being a top executive and political aide to the Governor. He wanted to move quickly. Word was that he had in mind appointing one of his deputies, a long-time career budget official, as Director of the new department, but had not made a final decision.

2. I knew that my Director and his political deputy also had a lot of influence in the administration. They would also be involved in the appointment decision because they would be turning over the Architecture division to the new department. I speculated that having recently and rather abruptly removed me from their team, they might be willing to help me relocate (if it would not interfere with their plans).

3. I had heard somewhere that if you want to get a particular job, announce that you want a higher one and then settle for the one you really want. It was not my usual style, but I felt that such a ploy might succeed in this case because I was generally seen as non-political, straightforward, and perhaps a bit too idealistic.

4. I went to the political deputy and said that I would like to become Director of the new General Services department. I said that I had become so committed to the Architecture division and so pleased with its progress that I wanted to go to the new department (in which architectural services

would be the largest function) rather than stay in the Transportation department. I asked for his support and that of the Director. He agreed to do what he could.

5. I phoned the leading candidate for Director of General Services (a long-time colleague) and told him what I had just done. I added, however, that I fully expected him to get the appointment anyway and if that happened I would be happy to become one of his two deputies and look after the Architecture division for him, and whatever else he might want me to do.

6. As soon as his appointment was announced, the newly-chosen Director called me to offer me a deputy director appointment (subject to the Governor's approval). The salary was higher than expected – a pleasant surprise. (I later learned that it was set on the basis of the other deputy appointment; I rode along on the basis that both deputies would be paid the same.)

Later, my former boss and friend, the political deputy, was heard to grouse (only partly joking, I think), "Hell, if I had known how much that job paid, I'd have taken a run for it myself." He had indeed done me a very large favor. Perhaps he thought I had earned it. Perhaps it was a bigger favor than he intended. Perhaps not. With him, I was never sure.

Chapter Nine

ADMINISTRATIVE SERVICES

THE IDEA OF having specialists provide various administrative services in organizations has been around for a long time. Recently, however, such specialists have multiplied amazingly.

The theory may have originated in the military doctrine of line and staff: combat troops are supported by staff units (personnel, materiel, intelligence, finance, etc.). Line units accomplish the mission; staff provides service to them. Staff units do not have command authority over line. Both line and staff report to a common commander, who is responsible for both.

In civilian management theory the same assumptions apply as in the military: (1) line executives will be freed to concentrate on the mission or program; (2) services will be more efficiently performed by specialists; (3) line officials retain at some level the authority to coordinate line and staff and to resolve any conflicts. The staff provides the means; the line accomplishes the ends. Staff specialists are supposed to be on tap, not on top

Unfortunately, it often does not work that way. In practice, the servants can often become the masters (at least within their specialties). Line executives, although theoretically in charge, find that each staff service establishes a complex web of rules and procedures which establish the "right way" to receive its services. Staff officials, preoccupied with their services, can easily lose sight of accomplishing the work for which the over-all organization exists. Means become more important than ends.

At the same time, it becomes easy for line officials to blame staff for shortcomings of their own operations. They may not know how to be good clients – to define clearly what is needed, to work cooperatively, to distinguish between optional and essential, to recognize the difference between good and bad staff work (and how to respond). Poor line clients are more likely to get poor staff service – the two reinforce each other's weaknesses.

Unfortunately, it may be tempting to staff people to assume and even to encourage ignorance of their special work. In the short run, it seems to make the staff more important and indispensable ("What would you do without me?"). An expert seems more impressive when you know little about what the person is doing. A client may be less likely to criticize service if convinced only specialists understand it. The uninformed client seems to have little choice ("Trust me, I know what I am doing and you don't" is the message the client receives.)

In larger organizations, staff services tend to multiply and to subdivide like reproducing cells. There are more specialties and more subspecialties. Instead of just a personnel service, we get specialists in job evaluation, recruiting, testing, performance review, training and development, salaries and wages, labor relations. More recently, we may also find affirmative action, communications, personnel computer systems, health benefits, sexual bias and harassment, and other newer subspecialties which cut across the personnel functions with specialized services to personnel staff.

Besides such increasing specialization, there are also continued additions to the classic staff functions. Personnel, finance, materiel, systems and, of course, law, are joined by such special services as public relations, publications, security, computer services, transportation, risk management, information. Whatever becomes the focus of increased concern – such as restructuring, corporate culture, downsizing, – is likely to become an added staff service.

The result of all this is often a sort of organizational Tower of Babel, in which the voice of management is nearly drowned out by a chorus of voices speaking many different "languages." Fewer people are able to communicate with one another fully and freely.

A likely response by line managers to all this increasing line-staff complexity is to equip themselves with staff specialists of their own – who can mediate between the generalists and the specialists, being able (the manager hopes) to speak both languages. Confronted, say, with computer systems specialists, it is not an unreasonable response to want an interpreter specialist of your own. The same need may arise in one specialty after another. Each "solution" adds to complexity and increases the difficulty of getting things done.

As more and more hinges are added to the billiard cue, it becomes more and more difficult for a player to get a straight shot.

All of this by way of background to explain why the State of California established (as had the Federal government a short time before) a Department of General Services. It was a response to the problems of rapidly growing staff services in a rapidly growing government. The hope was that if most of these services were put under one organizational tent, things might go better.

"Better" meant different things to different people. To those primarily interested in budget and related central management functions, the need was to enable the Finance department to concentrate on its role as the central management agency for the Governor, supporting the Governor as chief executive and providing management controls for him (or at least in his name). To those primarily interested as clients for other central services, the need was to improve quality, efficiency and responsiveness. They hoped that such units might operate more as a service (and less as a control) if taken out of the powerful finance agency. Others were neutral, feeling that the change in structure would make little difference.

As a deputy director of the new department, I was one of three people put in charge of establishing the new agency and making it work. How did reality compare with theory? The answers can be grouped under four headings:

- The resistance of inertia
- The power of service
- The need for a little inefficiency
- The need for better clients

1. The resistance of inertia. When a large organization is restructured, much more time and effort goes into just "keeping things going" and in making minor repairs and adjustments than is usually anticipated. The time and effort available for actually making the hoped-for changes which were the basic purpose of reorganization is usually much less than is expected.

What did change initially? There was a new piece of paper: the statute which created the department, its basic charter. A few "new" people (including me) were appointed – actually (as in my case) not so much "new" people but the same people in new leadership roles. A few relationships did start to change, both inside and outside the department, but the shifts were tentative at first. This was not a crisis reorganization, so people could feel freer to wait and see.

The mandate as we three "new" executives saw it was threefold: get the service functions out of Finance and Public Works departments; keep them going satisfactorily; improve the services. The first happened almost immediately. The second took most of everyone's attention, particularly during the first year or so. The third, not very well defined, largely awaited whatever time the new leadership could give it.

Daily routines always tend to leave little time for initiatives. A reorganization may establish important new goals, but it also raises a huge number of operating questions which demand immediate attention. As all these urgent administrative details are dealt with (arranging office space, revising directives, making new delegations, setting up new routines, etc.) the pressure is to leave operations running mostly the same as they have been (if there do not seem to be urgent issues). That wonderful first fresh moment of opportunity goes quickly, and it is easy to spend it changing details, continuing most of the past, and postponing most of the rest.

My feeling is that new structures do open up new possibilities, but that these still have to be identified and acted upon before anything significant happens. The reorganization does not do the job. Inside leadership or outside threat (or both) is needed to overcome inertia and initiate timely action. It is easier to picture beforehand what you would change if you could; it is harder to picture how you would keep things going as they are, develop real plans for change, and start things moving that way – all at the same time.

What happened in the case of the Architecture function illustrates what can happen when a new manager is able to follow up a reorganization with immediate attention to all three aspects. I had already spent several years being familiar with the division, its operations and its people. I already had some definite goals and knew how to set about moving toward them. I knew where there was support and where there might be problems. I also knew all the things I did not need to change (and fortunately there were a great many of them). The initial details and the business of keeping most things going were relatively simple in this case.

My first step was to make a symbolic change which sent an important message. I changed the name of the organization (with the Director's approval) from Architecture division to Office of Architecture and Construction. I had several things in mind. The construction function was important and widely admired by clients. Architecture was more than an architectural design shop, and I wanted to highlight that. It sounded more like an organization serving clients; "division" has a bureaucratic ring, and did not fit in the context of the new department. I wanted to emphasize that this was a new beginning in a new department with a new name – both to clients and to people in the organization. I wanted to set up positive expectations. And, yes, I wanted to show that I had the power and authority to make the change and was willing to use it. I was sending a message about myself as well as about the Division. (Changing a name can fit well with reorganization: it can be done quickly, costs little, carries large implications, and is not easy to oppose.)

2. The power of services. A paradox of traditional management is that it insists on the need for powerful managers in command of the organizational pyramid, but at the same time wants powerful staff services which are apt to inhibit and fragment that power. Line managers can end up having the authority while staff services have the power.

I do not believe that this paradox can be resolved by trying to draw a line sharply distinguishing between "pure" service functions, on the one hand, and "pure" line functions on the other. The way you do things is integrally bound up with what you are trying to do, and vice versa. Some activities may be done by line managers as part of their own work and in other cases are done by staff, depending on the situation.

It seems to me that the practicalities of power these days so favor the specialists (their number, prestige, professionalism, technology, jargon, access to top management, control of information) that renewed emphasis should be placed on their service role. Some specialties have quite completely escaped the advisory and service role and long since have become familiar instruments of central control in their own right: budget and finance, law, personnel, purchasing, information systems, etc.). Others aspire to the same prestige and power if conditions permit.

At the least, a partnership role (in which mutual interests and responsibilities are emphasized) would seem to make more sense. General managers need to be encouraged to seek this role, and staff service managers need to be encouraged to accept it. When we wonder why some organizations seem to find it hard to focus on accomplishing their mission, we might find some of the answer in the way we often give more real power to those who control the means than to those who labor toward the ends.

3. The need for a little inefficiency. This point is closely related to the preceding point. If staff services become too powerful and efficient, they may reduce the over-all performance of the organization. If each of the services were able to operate in the way they would consider ideal, the combined result would probably be an organization which performs its mission poorly.

Each specialist I have worked with can visualize how much better a job could be done with more time, more resources, more support for the particular service they perform. However, it is not hard to see that if program managers had to adjust to the many needs (not necessarily compatible with one another) of the many staff services, they would have little ability to manage operations.

Visualize a mansion in which the work of each of the servants is to be ideally efficient. The car can be used only at the convenience of the driver, and in ways which reduce the cost of operation to a minimum. The rooms are cleaned when it is efficient for the cleaners, regardless of the effect on occupants. Ultimately, it might seem most efficient not to have anyone live in the house — occupants tend to get in the way and make more work for the servants. Of course, some servants might still get in one another's way, so even then some might be able to work more efficiently than others.

Put in these terms, it seems clear that the efficiency of services makes sense only if and only to the extent that it meets the needs of the organization. It takes balance and awareness and mutual accommodation. To impose an over-all requirement on the staff services – that their basic task is still to help get the primary work of the organization done better, faster and less expensively – is a tough standard, but a sensible one.

4. The need for better clients. Even when staff specialists have a proper sense of balance and restraint, there is still another requirement: better clients. Good services also depend on good clients who play an active part in the relationship and understand how to get the help they need.

The role of client is not easy for some managers to understand. It does not fit the traditional concepts of command and subordinate roles. A client is neither fully in command nor fully dependent in relation to a service specialist. Rather than merely wishing for better clients or resorting to control tactics, service organizations need to make client education an active, essential part of their responsibilities.

A purchasing service, for example, needs to help its customers learn to define their needs for supplies and services in ways which clarify real requirements, yet leave appropriate room for purchasers to use their expert abilities. To know what an expert can do, a client may need help. A good client will contribute more to the service relationship, but is likely to expect more in return than a passive or reluctant or hostile client.

An example of this concept at work is a Good Design program which I started while deputy director of the General Services department. Its purpose was to help improve the quality of architectural services by educating clients. In order for State architects to do a better job, they needed clients who could define their functional needs better, understand architectural services, participate actively in the process, and support quality design work. That program is discussed further in the next chapter.

Chapter Ten

DESIGN

MOST MANAGERS ARE more verbal than visual, but design of the work environment can be a tool of management. Unfortunately, managerial interest in design is often limited to those aspects which enhance the prestige of the executives.

The Governor's Good Design program in State government originated specifically as a way to further improve architectural services to State agencies, which was one of my management goals as a deputy director in the General Services department.

It was in part a straightforward training program – an effort to help the architects by training their clients. It also carried important messages to State executives: good design is important; it is not incompatible with economy; obtaining it is in part a management responsibility. The program used Californians from architectural and other design fields (a visible sign of new public-private partnership). It put the Governor in a favorable personal role: active supporter of excellence in design.

I started with a few key ideas. First, I felt that design as a concept applied to much more than buildings. It included all kinds of designed structures (highways, bridges, water projects, etc.) and outdoor environments. It included the design of graphic communication, (such as signs, publications, forms, letterheads, logos). It included the design of interior spaces (offices, furniture, exhibits). By broadening the concept of design, one could enlarge the audience and increase the impact of the subject – going beyond any one design specialty or group.

Second, by involving the Governor personally, as official sponsor, we could attract support from his top officials and obtain participation by outstanding and talented people in the various fields of design at little or no cost. A personal invitation from the Governor usually obtained a favorable response.

Third, it needed to be a continuing program, not a one-time single event. We developed several complementary parts for the program: a Governor's Conference in Good Design, for initial impact and attention (Governor as keynote speaker); Design Workshops, as follow-up training for managers (using both outside experts and State officials); a Governor's Advisory Committee on Good Design, to help make good design a lasting policy (again, a mix of experts and officials); a Governor's Design Awards Program to recognize and honor outstanding design in California with annual awards (certificates publicly presented by the Governor); further Governor's Conferences on Good Design, to focus on other areas of design (such as transportation or environment); further Design Training, for State employees. I intended to build all these elements into the established policies and structures of the new department and of State government, because it would take years to get all the hoped-for results.

Fourth, by involving outstanding private design professionals in the program along with State officials and employees, I could improve relations between the two – working against the stereotypes of both. Also, such participation builds its own momentum: as you get some top people to accept, it becomes easier to get others.

Fifth, as deputy director, I could take actions which would specifically demonstrate some of the design policies being advocated.

1. Two large new office buildings were being planned for downtown Sacramento in the capitol area – a major project. The preliminary design (prepared earlier, before the reorganization) was poor (heavy and unattractive, a high-rise bunker). As client for the building (General Services provided general office space for State agencies), I rejected the design and asked for something better. Later, when the re-design still needed some refinement, I hired a top private firm as architectural consultants – partly to improve design details, partly to protect our staff architects and their design from harm during fiscal reviews, and partly to exemplify public-private partnership.

2. In the construction budget for the new office project, I included funds for public art – a sculpture for the plaza

which would adjoin the two buildings. With the help of the project architects, a competition was held.

3. The competition was won by Bruce Beasley, a young sculptor in Oakland, who used the money to develop a method of casting large sculptures in clear acrylic, which he went on to use in many other sculpture works. The cost of the art was so minor in relation to the $20 million project that it was hardly noticed – yet the impact was considerable. (Later, including such public art funding in projects became more widespread, but at the time it was rare.)

4. A new Master Plan had recently been completed by the Capitol Building and Planning Commission, and the State was purchasing much of the site. I located the office buildings project so as to anchor one corner of the Master Plan and give it some immediate reality.

5. A private engineering firm was designing a central heating and cooling plant to provide for present and future State needs in the capitol area. It would be near the two new high-rise office buildings. When I saw their preliminary design for the plant building (windowless black tile walls and two curved metal entry ramps), I suggested that design of the plant building be turned over to the State architectural staff. The redesign was a simple structure which related in materials and design to the new office buildings across the street. Through glass walls on all four sides, one could see the huge machines, their elements color coded: red for heating, blue for cooling, etc. (Later, on a hunch, I asked our architects to check the engineering design of air vents for the distribution tunnels which would extend throughout the Capitol area. Again, without affecting cost or function, the vents were made simple and inconspicuous.)

6. The standard stationery for State agencies was printed by the General Services department – at the time, it featured versions of the State seal and rather traditional type faces

> and layouts. A rising graphic design firm in San Francisco agreed to lend the State at no cost a couple of staff people who would develop some better-designed alternatives. (They would have been very willing to redesign the State seal, too, but I was afraid to tackle that one – perhaps an opportunity was missed. They did prepare some redesigned agency logos, just to show the possibilities.)

The process by which this rather extensive program was developed is as interesting as the design concepts, and in terms of management perhaps as unconventional.

Consider the situation: no budget for the program; an abstract and somewhat elitist-sounding topic (good design); no established major contacts with the special worlds of various design professionals; a tradition in State government that dull inexpensive-looking design was safest and therefore best.

Consider also, however, some advantages. I understood State government and how it worked, I had status as a Governor-appointee, and wide latitude from my Director to work mostly on my own. The subject was non-political, but could give the Governor a new and positive message (which would probably be welcome in the second year of his second four-year term). I remembered Cyril Magnin, with whom I had worked briefly in a study of the San Francisco Port, whose board he had chaired at the time. He was a business leader, a well-known public benefactor, a supporter of the Governor. It was the Cyril Magnin connection and his immediate support and advice which made all the rest possible.

Magnin put me in touch with Nathaniel Owings, a founding partner of Skidmore, Owings and Merrill, who headed the San Francisco office of the large national architectural firm. At this stage in a distinguished career he was interested in volunteer public service activities (He was at the time, among other things, chairing an advisory group for President Kennedy to redesign Pennsylvania Avenue in the national capitol). Owings agreed to chair the Advisory Committee on Good Design and to recruit members.

Soon, he (and Magnin) were joined on the Board by other distinguished people: another prominent architect, the Dean of the

UC Berkeley School of Environmental Design, the director of a famous lithography studio. Others accepted invitations to be on the program of the Governor's Design Conference: a noted designer of furniture, interiors, graphics, exhibits and films; an innovative designer of corporate graphics and products; the architectural and design curator of the Museum of Modern Art in New York; and others, equally stars in their fields.

These people donated their time because of the personal prestige of the people who contacted them, the assurances from them that the program was worthy of their support, and the perception (through them) that it was an opportunity to influence California government policy toward design.

As a practical matter, they were also assured that their participation would require only limited time and effort. They wanted to participate directly, not be a mere letterhead group, but they also needed to be sure their cameo roles would be brief and easy.

Meanwhile, I was contributing several less conspicuous but equally essential things on behalf of State government. As deputy director, I could provide (1) access to State funding; (2) State employee staff help; a Planning Committee of State people, which I chaired. (The Director of General Services was Conference Chairman.)

The matter of money was crucial. Nat Owings found this the most surprising aspect of the whole process. He said that the usual problem in dealing with governments was that no matter how promising the idea, somebody would usually say "Sorry, but we don't have the money," and that would put an end to it. I, on the other hand, was able to say, "You get the people for us and keep us on the right track, and I'll see that we have the money."

Actually, money was somewhat of a problem, but one I felt I could solve. There was a mechanism available: the overhead and administrative costs related to State building projects were ultimately charged in the accounting system to the projects. With all the free outside help we were getting and the uncharged time of people in State government, our cash costs for the program were not large. When publications, meeting rooms, travel and other such expenses had to be paid, they could be merged with other overhead charges and split among many projects. The financial effect on any one project was small.

I also had in mind – and was willing to risk acting on it – that with such high-level sponsorship, nobody would question this method of financing, especially if the program was a success. The sad thing, perhaps, is how seldom public service provides the circumstances where such entrepreneurial initiative is feasible.

The other managerial element I provided was intellectual rigor. As initiator and manager of the program, I had clearly in mind certain ideas and goals. I could make sure that all elements of the program remained integrally related. The many people involved in the effort had a lot of flexibility to approach their parts in their own way. However, the cumulative impact was strong because all these elements related back to the basic themes and messages.

For example, while the Governor's keynote speech at the Conference was drafted by his staff, I provided lots of material and suggestions. The result was a joint product – better than I could have written, but still targeted appropriately as the keynote of the whole program. Once the Governor said it, it could be quoted and used as policy.

That was my best role: I understood what we were trying to do and I knew how we were trying to do it. I cared about every aspect. I never let the program lose its focus as it grew into a far-flung undertaking.

It was also one of the most enjoyable experiences of my whole career – a high point which is still fresh in my mind.

How did it turn out? The Governor's Conference on Good Design was all I had hoped for and more. The Sacramento newspapers described two hundred state executives as "bubbling with excitement." My boss reported that the Governor was excited and pleased and would give his continued support. The outside participants reported that the Conference was attracting national attention and causing similar efforts to be initiated elsewhere,

Once I floated back down from the clouds, we continued during the next six months with well-attended Design Workshops covering the whole range of design, using both design professionals and State training specialists.

Did it make a difference? Yes, I think so. You can never measure it, but I felt there was a definite shift in prevailing attitudes. Several agencies picked up on the ideas and used them to improve their work. Design of some freeways, bridges and water projects improved. The design of State buildings continued to get better.

On the negative side, I probably should have kept on more aggressively to keep the momentum going and to build it somehow more firmly into State practices. The program still tended to move only when I pushed. It was to the end more my program than the State government's – and some patient bureaucrats no doubt counted on this all along.

When Governor Brown's term ended and I moved on, the Good Design program disappeared. I think of two bits of further symbolism about the program. First, on the very day of the Conference, when the Governor was proclaiming a sort of renaissance in the State's approach to civic design, he was called away to deal with reports of riots in Sproul Plaza at UC Berkeley. It was the first dramatic spark of the explosive campus disruptions which were eventually so damaging to the Governor's administration. (Sometimes the things that happen to you unexpectedly just overwhelm the things you were planning.)

The second image is more personal for me. After the Governor had lost the election and was within days of the end of his term, I flew with him to Pasadena in his National Guard plane. At a ceremony there, he publicly presented the long-planned Governor's Awards for good design. Somehow, none of the people who usually traveled with the Governor could make it on this day. It seemed to me a good way to mark the end of the Good Design Program and to show my appreciation to the Governor for having made it possible.

Chapter Eleven

TECHNOLOGY

NEW TECHNOLOGY HAS a particular impact on management, sometimes positive, sometimes negative, usually both. New technology is marketed to managers as an indispensable management tool (whether it is or not). Left unsaid by the marketers is the fact that the new tool will require managers to change the way their organizations operate. It is often difficult to distinguish between "Here's a new tool which does something that you need and does it better" and "Here's a new gadget which you need because it is new, so surely you can find a way to use it."

The late fifties and early sixties were a time in which some of the technology we now think of as defining contemporary work organizations had its beginnings. Because government is such a large purchaser, it is an attractive marketing target. Contrary to common belief, State government at the time was an early and eager user of technological innovations. Copy machines made an early appearance in government offices – Xerox and 3M, replacing carbon paper, mimeo and ditto – on their way to becoming ubiquitous. The electric typewriter began as a prestige item for executive secretaries and worked its way into every government office.

Other changes were more gradual, but no less dramatic in impact. The move from operator-manned manual telephone switchboards to automatic dial systems was as much a social change as a change in technology. It took major marketing to get people used to answering their own direct-dialed phones at their individual telephone number. (Managers were more willing to impose the change because most of them still had secretaries to screen their calls.)

Similarly, elevator operators disappeared as elevators became automatic (although for years operators still pushed the buttons of the automatic elevators which served legislators in the capitol building). Fluorescent lights changed the ceilings of offices everywhere to panels of light (often greenish and flickering) which people were taught to leave on day and night. Office furniture changed from oak to metal (except in the executive suites). Wall-to-wall carpet, at first reserved for executive suites, was eventually accepted as the basic floor covering for most general office space. Long distance calls changed from a special-expense item, approved in advance by supervisors, to become as routine as local calls. Airplane travel replaced trains, and motor pools handled the rest.

A good case could be made that these heavily-marketed changes in the technology of communication, travel and the office were as important (perhaps more important) in the evolution of management than the changes in management theory. The resources for marketing such products and for overcoming customer resistance were far greater than was available to management researchers and teachers. The temper of the times favored technological progress and expected it to be the basis of a better future.

Of all the changes, however, the one with the greatest impact was the computer. It serves as a specific example of technological response in State government. Again, government was an early and enthusiastic user. It had the volume of transactions and records, the background in punched-card data processing, the standardized systems, and the rapid growth rate which made early computer applications feasible – expensive, awkward, and often stumbling, but still, feasible.

As the technology moved beyond this early period, large-scale computer systems proliferated throughout State agencies. During the early 1960's, the State administration entered into several contracts with various California aerospace companies to study the application of aerospace technology to State operations. The motivation was basically political: aerospace companies were in a slump, and needed new customers; the State administration wanted to help an important California industry and to be seen as using leading-edge technology to improve government. The State offered cooperation and contracts; the aerospace firms offered consultants at lower-than-usual rates. The contracts in effect invited them to develop proposals.

Whether or not any actual applications resulted from these consulting contracts was less important than their immediate visibility. Just announcing the program and letting the contracts was enough to reap considerable benefits.

Of the four or five such projects, the one I was most involved in dealt with computers and information systems and was handled by Lockheed. Lockheed supplied a team of engineering consultants from its own workforce. The State supplied a Governor's task force, composed of State managers and staff. I was a member of this task force.

It was, I think, this interaction between the outside consultants and the inside client group which made this particular study interesting. The outside specialists were experienced in computer information systems for an entirely different environment, but they were also used to relating to government clients. The State group provided what some of the other studies lacked: an active and knowledgeable client group with whom to interact.

Like most such groups, the State task force was an ad hoc group. Its members (and the staff people who helped) simply found time to participate in addition to doing their regular jobs, with no additional compensation. They did it because of interest in the project or because they were assigned by their bosses or both. It was at the time a widely used device in State government for bringing together appropriate mixes of talents and interests to focus for a limited time on some problem or area. It enabled people to work together outside the usual hierarchy and channels on a common task. When its task was done, the group disbanded.

The interaction of task force and consultant group continued through the study and then, when the report was issued, extended to developing proposed State legislation based on the report. In the process, the recommendations were modified to make them more feasible and acceptable in State government.

The proposal was a master plan for a Statewide Federated Information System (SFIS), an electronic information network for State government. Even then (thirty years ago) the computer-based information systems already established separately had the potential of being linked, so that data could be accessed and moved between systems. The existing systems dealt with separate programs (employment, finance, resources, enforcement, vehicles). The report indicated that evolving technology would enable them to become in some respects one system.

The conventional wisdom of the time, which saw computers as ever-larger giant machines, would have been to attempt to centralize all these operating data systems or to create a central integrated computer information system. While technologically feasible, apparently, the State group felt this approach would be impractical and unwise – incompatible with the rather loose and sprawling structure of State government and its need to keep operations decentralized. It also raised questions of privacy, citizen protection, and data confidentiality in relation to such a monolithic system.

The proposal which emerged from the joint study was for a Federated information system – that is, the data would remain in the various computer operating systems, but there would be a sort of central computer catalog or locater system through which one could find where various items of information were kept and have access to them. The system would be federated, meaning that its members would each retain control of their own data and operations while participating in the joint information exchange system. It would be Statewide in the sense that local governments would be able to join in the system.

The SFIS would be a facilitating service, not an information control center. To make this workable, certain minimum technical standards would have to be adopted. Without preventing competition among computer vendors, the standards would provide the necessary compatibility in hardware and software.

It was visionary, it was ahead of its time, it was (like most long-range plans) far from fully developed. It was not exactly what either the aerospace or the State group had had in mind earlier (which, to me, was one of its most promising features). It seemed to make a different kind of sense of the explosive growth of State computer systems.

The administration did sponsor legislation which would establish the SFIS and its basic policies. As it happened, I wound up becoming a principal presenter for the administration when the proposed legislation came up for hearing in legislative committee. Not being an expert, I tried to find simple metaphors and common-sense explanations. I'm not sure they would always have struck the experts as accurate – something, for instance about establishing standard gauge for the rails of a system being built piecemeal, so that eventually cars could roll throughout the railroad network.

The legislation did not pass that year, but there was enough positive response that I felt "maybe next year" was a reasonable hope. By this time, State government had master plans for highways, higher education, water, the capitol, etc. – why not a master plan for a Statewide Federated Information System, too. It seemed possible to me. (You need to realize that at that time, "master plan" was as good a word as "technology" and "progress" and "growth" and "future" – hard to believe, today.

The moment passed, unseized. By the next legislative session, the SFIS proposal had been swept away by the flood of political events and the idea was forgotten. There was a different Governor and a different administration. I was no longer involved in information system plans in any way. (It's enough to keep a manager humble about foreseeing the future.)

The computer revolution in State government continued anyway, but without the benefit (or handicap) of an information system master plan.

Chapter Twelve

CONFLICT AND RESISTANCE

THE TOOLS OF management are used both for offense and for defense. So much of management deals with avoiding conflict and controversy that it is easy to overlook the importance of negative management. Managers do try to make things happen, get things done, exercise leadership – all those positive things. Managers also try to make things not happen, keep things from being done, lead in opposition, defend against attacks. Managers are as concerned with keeping things going the way they are as with bringing about changes.

A small case from my own experience: the Father Serra controversy. At first, it was not a controversy but simply a piece of legislation. The State legislature passed a law authorizing the placing of a statue of Father Junipero Serra, one of the founders of the California mission system, in Capitol Park. The financing was to be from private sources.

The bill had been passed and signed into law before I heard of it. One day the Director of General Services handed me a copy, said that the law made the department responsible for carrying it out, and asked me to look after it.

With a little asking around, the background became clear. The Catholic Church in California had a long-term goal of having Father Serra declared a saint by the Pope. One of several criteria was the extent to which the candidate has achieved widespread and lasting fame for his or her achievements. Evidence of fame could include, among other things, public statues.

The priest who was in charge of advocating Serra's sainthood (apparently a lifetime assignment) had joined with representatives of the Native Sons and the Native Daughters of the Golden West as joint sponsors. There were, of course, already many statues of Serra in California, but one placed in such a prominent and prestigious location would further honor him and help the sainthood cause.

With the support of the Governor and several legislative leaders, the bill had been non-controversial and had passed easily. (There were already other monuments of California history in the Capitol and in the surrounding park, gifts from various groups. A statue of Columbus and Isabella had long stood in the center of the Capitol building rotunda, a monument not so much to California history as to the importance of Italian -Americans and their explorer hero. Such gifts had a long tradition – what could be controversial about another one?)

It was only as I learned in more detail what the donors had in mind that the project became controversial – first of all, in my own mind. The law did not specify the location or describe the appearance of the statue, and left it to the department to approve both. The priest advocate, however, made it very plain at our first meeting that in his mind this was already settled: (1) location – directly in front of the main entrance to the Capitol building; (2) appearance – a heroic larger-than-life Serra, holding a very large Christian cross and raising his other hand in blessing (as sketched by the already-chosen artist).

It seemed to me that the project was controversial from two standpoints: mediocre as art and inappropriate as a Catholic icon. I had no doubt that once this statue appeared in such an enormously prominent location there would be a belated public outcry. Art critics would regard it as bad art. Those concerned that church and state be kept separate would regard it as bad public policy. I could picture people turning to me and saying, "Why did you let this happen? It is your fault!"

At the same time, I felt that I had no power to reject the project in the face of the political and legal support it had already received. The sponsors were determined and obviously had their minds closed. It seemed plain to me that neither the Governor nor the legislative sponsors would want to have the matter put back in their hands.

What I needed was a controversy – not a controversy between me and the sponsors (which I would surely lose), but a controversy which would make the stature "controversial" so that without taking sides I could call a halt. It would not be my decision; I would merely be responding to the controversy and forced to wait until it had been resolved.

In search of controversy, I first tried to interest the Capitol Building and Planning Commission in reviewing the project. They were responsible for checking construction projects in relation to the Capitol area master plan. They declined to become involved.

Next, I undertook to establish a review group specifically for the Serra project. I phoned the chairs of the art departments at nearby university and college campuses and invited them to serve on an advisory art committee. I explained that (1) I did not feel qualified to review the project from an artistic standpoint, (2) we wanted to be sure the project would be of high quality, and (3) the committee work would not take much time. To the committee I also appointed the priest and the pioneer group representatives of the sponsoring organizations. I'm not sure, but I think I may also have included an architect. It was all very quick and informal.

The first meeting of the advisory committee was, as it turned out, the only meeting. I did not attend (not wanting to seem to influence the group one way or another) but I sent someone from my staff to serve as secretary. According to the report I received back, the meeting was short and stormy. The art professors looked at the project, hated it, and said so with considerable clarity. The sponsors were outraged and responded with considerable heat. The meeting soon broke up in disagreement and anger.

It was clear to me that the project had become controversial. I notified the sponsors that under the circumstances we could not proceed. I put it away for six months or so, without further contact with anyone.

My objective, however, was not to block the project permanently. I wanted the sponsors to become flexible enough that the whole approach could be reconsidered. Their overriding goal was to have a Serra monument. If it took changes in location and design in order to accomplish this, I felt they would eventually be willing to accept them.

After enough time had gone by, I asked one of our best staff architects to consider what might appropriately be done. He came back with a new approach: (1) location – a park site behind the Capitol, surrounded by a grove of camellias; (2) appearance – a bronze relief map of California, set nearly flat on the lawn; a less-than-lifesize Serra statue, holding a very small cross and looking down at the missions marked on the map; (3) setting – the map and statue were set within a circular walkway; embedded in the walk were bronze plaques, showing the building and the date of each California mission.

It was not great art, but it was several other things: (1) in compliance with the statute; (2) an educational history exhibit; (3) reasonably attractive; (4) in a beautiful secluded park setting; (5) unlikely to be controversial; and (6) in keeping with the basic interests of the sponsors.

I offered the new proposal to the sponsors and they reluctantly approved it. Their sculptor got to do the statue, smaller and reconceived. Our architects did the rest of the design and supervised construction. I never went back to the advisory group. It had served its function and, with the passage of time, had faded away. I did not want to risk a new controversy.

It is there today in Capitol Park, the Father Serra California Mission monument. It has aged well and fits quietly into the landscape. I understand that it is popular with school groups who visit the State Capitol. (The missions are a major topic for fourth graders in California schools.)

Just to balance the scales, let me give a second example of the use of conflict. This, too, was a Capitol controversy – created for a purpose, quickly forgotten when its purpose had been served, leaving some lasting effects – but this one was aimed straight at me.

The Capitol building was being repainted – the wood and metal parts, that is. The lower part is grey granite of two shades. The rest of the wedding-cake structure is of wood with metal classic columns and details, all painted white. On top of the building is a large metal dome (somewhat in the style of the national capitol, but on a smaller scale).

The question was the dome: how should it be finished? Although most people thought of it as California's "golden" Capitol dome, it was in fact made of copper sheathing which had weathered to the dull greenish patina of copper long exposed to the air.

Ideally, the dome would have been covered with gold leaf. However, after testing several methods, the architects concluded that to do so would be very difficult and very expensive. They recommended the dome be painted white (like the national capitol dome) as part of the exterior painting work.

I was well aware that any major change in the appearance of the Capitol building could arouse controversy. I took care to present the recommendation to the joint legislative committee which had charge of the building. They approved painting the dome white. The chair provided me with a letter of authorization and we put out a request for painting bids.

The next thing I knew, my boss (the Director of General Services) was on the phone demanding to know what was happening to the Capitol dome. His phone was ringing off the hook with calls from media all over the state and from the Governor's staff as well. There was, it seemed, a tidal wave of negative reaction to a white-painted dome. "California deserves a gold dome" seemed the message of the day.

The public controversy lasted about a week – a very difficult, uncomfortable week. My wife, a native of both California and Sacramento, had warned me. The Capitol dome should be gold, she said, and most people think it already is. They are not going to like the idea of painting it white. (Actually, there was some gold on the dome, but it was a little gold (or possibly gold-plated) ball atop the dome, not the dome itself.)

The controversy seemed to feed on itself, as the media got quotes from every conceivable interest group: historic, financial, political, artistic, civic, etc. Elected officials quickly ran for cover: cancel the request for bids; make a study; see what gold leaf would cost; hold everything; reconsider everything.

Later, I found out how all this had started. The news release about the painting bids had reached the Capitol newsroom on a particularly dull and quiet news day. Somebody spotted it and wondered if a controversy could be started so as to make some news. Several of the journalists agreed to give it a try. They got on the phones and raised the Capitol-dome-should-be-white-or-gold question with as many people as they could reach. They hit a real nerve. Everybody had an opinion on this, and was ready to express it.

Soon the storm blew over, and the media moved on to other news. What was the result? Not a gold dome, not a white dome, but a no-change as-is dome: ever since then (for more than 25 years), the dome has continued with its greenish copper patina unchanged except by the weather. Nobody has wanted to pay for the gold. Nobody has wanted to sponsor the white paint.

During that time the entire Capitol building has been gutted, rebuilt and restored to its turn-of-the-century elegance, but the covering of the dome has remained unchanged. Perhaps it was based on the idea of restoration – the dome never had been golden, or white. Perhaps a copper patina is better than paint. I believe, however, that nobody has wanted to risk controversy by raising the issue. In any event, it shows once again that – intended or not – the result of controversy is often no action at all.

One last thought about conflict and controversy. They are surely used sometimes as a tool of management. They are also sometimes used as an anti-management tool, to delay and to block managerial action. However, increased conflict and controversy are being experienced today by managers in all kinds of organizations. The change seems to me to be not so much intentional as an unexpected side-effect of another change in managing.

Both internally and externally, as everything has become more and more specialized, we find structured representation of more and more viewpoints. Within organizations, there are more staff specialists who represent special viewpoints. Within operating units, there is often more encouragement of competition. In normal times, at least, managers are encouraged to allow participation in decision-making instead of ruling by fiat. Outside interests are increasingly likely to be represented by a constellation of groups, who demand to be heard.

The result of this increased participation is not so much broader consensus as more controversy, with its predictable outcomes: delay and stalemate. Some of this may well be used by managers to regain some authority ("Since you all disagree, I'll just have to decide it myself."), but most of it I think just eventually overwhelms managers and non-managers alike with a sense of frustration ("Why can't anyone get anything done around here?").

Participation does not guarantee consensus. Opening the doors to more different views is generally healthy, but only if the controversy it invites leads not to inaction but to better action. Otherwise, all concerned may be worse off than before.

Confronted more and more with conflict, managers should try to understand what needs underlie the controversies, to use that understanding in developing more appropriate solutions, and to act decisively when the time is right.

As for the Serra statue controversy, I have thought more recently of another possible interpretation. To me it was a question of using controversy first to block and then to modify the project. To the long-persevering advocates of sainthood for Serra (who still remain active in the cause, after all these years), it may seem that although secular authority at first blocked the Serra project, some higher power intervened to cause it to be completed. That would be another way of looking at it, I suppose.

Chapter Thirteen

ELECTIONS

MANAGERS CAN BECOME so comfortable in an organization – so familiar with how it works, so adept at using it to make things happen, so comfortable – that they forget how fragile and temporary their work world really is, how abruptly and unexpectedly it can shift as a result of changes in the larger social and political environment. When things are stable and going well, it feels as if you are managing things. Suddenly the whole situation changes and you are reminded that things are managing you, instead.

That happened to me in California State government, when a funny thing happened on the way to the polls. I did not see it coming. The Brown administration (of which I was a part) seemed to be losing energy. Having initiated so many plans and programs, there seemed after nearly eight years to be fewer things it wanted to accomplish and more things it wanted to protect. The voters seemed a little disenchanted with continued growth and taxes.

Nevertheless, when someone told me that a Southern California Republican group was planning to back the actor Ronald Reagan for Governor, I said (thinking of Governor Brown's political experience and years in office), "Reagan seems just the sort of candidate the Governor will do well against." It seemed plausible at the time.

What I didn't see then (but came to see during the election campaign) was a fundamental shift in Republican strategy. Governors Warren and Knight had been in the California tradition of progressive good government (with election contests more between individuals than between parties). Brown was more partisan, but still in the tradition which believed that government (especially local and State) provided necessary and important social and economic services. In general, such leaders proposed that government do more and do it better for the ultimate benefit of all citizens.

Suddenly, here was Reagan saying persuasively that government was the problem, not the solution. Instead of looking at social problems as a basis for developing public programs and solutions,

Reagan blamed government for the problems. His promise was to reduce taxes and reduce government in order to free individuals and businesses from an unfair and unnecessary burden. He suggested that you could spend your money better than the government could. In seeking to become Governor, he ran against the government.

With continued inflation, taxes in California had been rising more or less routinely. To those who wanted to halt or roll back the increase, Reagan said that tax revenues were not made necessary by government programs, but vice versa – expenditures rise to meet available tax revenues. His solution: limit or reduce taxes and you both limit government expenditures and keep more for yourselves and for the private economy. Taxes and government were bad; profits and private expenditures were good. Business meant enterprise and economic growth, government meant bureaucracy and waste.

These ideas were not all new, nor was Reagan their only advocate. He packaged them with such an appealing and reassuring personality, however, that they did not sound extreme. In the election, even Sacramento districts where State employees were concentrated were carried by Reagan. They did not see his attack on government as being directed at them. They were just making another routine voting choice between individuals, I think. In fact the election was a watershed change in public attitudes toward government.

I was surprised when Reagan was elected, but I was not surprised at the sweeping consequences. What did surprise me most was the number of my State employee friends who said to me after the election, "Of course, this isn't going to make any difference in our department, is it?" To which I could only reply, "Everything in State government is going to be different. It will take time, but everything will be different."

My immediate personal options were either to sit tight and see how long I could remain as deputy director or to return voluntarily to my civil service job of assistant director in the Public Works department and see what might develop.

I chose to resign and return to civil service. As a matter of principle, officials of the new administration were entitled to have from Governor-appointees a resignation which they could accept when and if they chose. I preferred to face the issue of my future sooner rather than later. Within a few days, I had met my successor and was back in my old job.

What all this means in terms of management is that you cannot manage the larger context in which you work. You can manage one project after another, and feel that you have made a difference. You can develop long-range plans and hope you will be around to implement them. You can be optimistic and confident, as you need to be.

At the same time it is healthy to keep in mind all the things beyond your control. Everything you are trying to do, everything you have built, everything you believe in – all these can be swept away by sudden changes. You need to keep it in the back of your mind as one possibility, and think a little about how you would respond if it should happen.

Besides my basic unpreparedness for the voter-initiated political upheaval, I found two other things particularly unexpected: the emotional impact of reentering civil service and the surprise of an unsolicited new job possibility.

It was no surprise that I would have to adjust to a more limited role. I was ready for that. It was no surprise that I would need to re-earn the trust of civil service colleagues. That made sense. What was unexpected was that I had enjoyed the excitement and the challenge of my political job. It was not a matter of prestige or power, but of work satisfaction. I could go back to the old job, but I was not sure how long I would find it satisfying.

This feeling was strong enough that I had already taken steps to explore going part-time to graduate school to work for a PhD in public administration at the nearby UC Davis campus. A doctorate would open the possibility of full-time university or college teaching.

It was a good plan, but it became moot when I received a phone call from a colleague at the University of California in Berkeley – a business administration professor who had served in the Brown administration and was now a Vice President in the Systemwide headquarters of the nine-campus University of California. He asked whether I would be interested in the position of Director of Business Services, working for him in Berkeley. I immediately said that

I was interested. (Plans are all very well, but sometimes your career just happens.)

By this time I had been in State government for over twenty years. It is somewhat unusual to leave voluntarily after long service, particularly from agencies which (like the State government) have good retirement plans. After a certain time, most people are held hostage by retirement benefits. You get to a point where you would lose a great deal in eventual retirement benefits if you left the system early. Normally, the longer you stay the less feasible it is to leave.

However, in California, the limitation had some loopholes. In order to increase mobility in public service careers, employees could move among State government, many local governments, and the University of California and have it count for retirement purposes as one single continuous employment. For me, the University of California could be considered because, first of all, I would not lose retirement benefits in moving there. (Such factors need to be an important part of individual career decisions.)

Looking back, the decision to accept the University of California job (when it was eventually offered) seems obvious. At the time, the future looked much more uncertain and the decision much more difficult.

One thing that happens with management decisions (and with career choices, which are an aspect of self-management), is that a lot of roads are not taken. You have to develop alternatives and possibilities in the process of finding what seems, all things considered, the best choice at the time.

It is not so important to keep looking back and trying to guess whether some other path would have led to some better result. What counts, I think, is the process – the willingness to search for non-obvious options, to keep more than one possibility open, to seize the unexpected. Later, if the results are good, it will seem to have been a rather simple decision and the other options, important at the time, will probably have faded away. Even if results are not what you hoped, you probably cannot be sure whether you had a better choice. (Management is primarily forward-looking; you can learn from the past, but you live in the present and the future.)

For example, I have never regretted leaving State government when I did. It was a considerable leap – from public administration to university administration, from staid Sacramento to lively Berkeley life, from the Reagan-demoralized civil service to the stimulating university service, from regretting the changes imposed from outside to welcoming the changes I had sought by my own choice. There were risks, but they seemed manageable.

What would have happened if I had made some other choice? It is not possible for me to know. Once the move was made, I did not look back much. It felt good that once again my family and I had taken the initiative, rather than waiting to see what might happen. (Just like a manager, you might say.)

PART THREE

UNIVERSITY MANAGEMENT

Snapshot (1970)

BY THIS TIME, we had been through the sixties in every sense. Sometimes it seemed as if the world was coming apart. The picture is still of a family – but an extending family which includes two teenagers and a twentysomething, one in high-school and two away at college. It was, as the saying goes, both the best and the worst of times.

The parts just didn't fit together as they used to. I was managing in a beleaguered university system – one still propelled by growth and the excitement of innovative new campuses, but under attack from student activists as the handy symbol of establishment repression and from Governor Reagan as the handy symbol of misguided liberal tolerance.

Somewhere along the way, many in the baby boom generation had decided that higher education and careers were a threat to a free lifestyle. To the accompaniment of appropriate music, clothes and mass gatherings, they were experimenting with new satisfactions, on the verge of dropout or beyond. Parents tried to keep in touch as best they could, feeling disoriented and fearful.

My wife, a social worker, was spending her days in the Black Panther realms of East Oakland, where alienation and anger and violence of a different kind were welling up amid the poverty. For her, the move between family life and work each day was a big shift; the move to the role of executive spouse at University social events was a jarring change of worlds. It was too much.

Meanwhile, Reagan and Nixon and other politicians were using the excesses of the young, the protests of the anti-war groups, the fears of the middle class, and the dislike of taxes to win elections. As they promised to win internal and external wars, to cut back social programs, to unleash business, they cast liberals and universities and governments as the enemy.

There I was – a liberal government bureaucrat in a famously liberal public university in a city whose name symbolized all that conservatives feared. And there I was also, typecast by Berkeley radicals as part of the system they were trying to overthrow, a far-over-thirty square scorned by the hippie culture. How could I suddenly have become so many different targets for so many different groups?

Of course, a lot of that was more rhetoric than real. We had come to Berkeley partly because it was a stimulating, exciting place both for us and our youngsters. In the midst of everything, I think all of us were glad to be where we were. Somehow we managed never to lose touch with each other.

If I think of an image of the time, I think of us – all five of us – driving across the country in the summer of 1970 in a Volkswagen bus which we had equipped with benches, pads, pillows and a roof rack. I had spent a month at Harvard Business School studying educational management, and we drove back from Boston to Berkeley in our tie-dyed T-shirts and our jeans and our funky bus. Our long-haired kids may have felt like 1960's nomads on the open road; to my wife and me, it still felt like the classic wonderful American family vacation – all of us together.

Chapter Fourteen

TRANSITIONS

ALL MANAGEMENT WORK involves transitions to some extent. Things never stay the same. Sometimes you are trying to make changes happen. Sometimes you are trying to keep things as they are in the face of changes. Sometimes you find that you are going through personal changes. Understanding the impact of changes and some ways of smoothing the change process can be useful for anyone – manager or not.

This particular change was a particular kind of transition: moving from one organization to another, and from one managerial post to another. If you think of large organizations as mountains, the image of transition from one to another is of a prodigious leap from one peak to another. The trick is to do it safely and with poise. (Management literature offers surprisingly little guidance on how to assume a new executive post.)

It helps to be very clear about why you are making the transition. In this case, it was not a choice between making a change or not. Whether I stayed or moved, there would be a major transition. I cared about the university, and could make a commitment to it as strong as the one I had made earlier to State government. The University's reputation was at this point very high. It was under attack. I felt I could help keep it strong and free. I hoped I could continue my career there for a long time.

What of the possible disadvantages? I was so drawn to making the move that I probed this less deeply, but certainly there were some obvious problems. Its size, structure, and concept of management were disadvantages.

The University was very big – "the General Motors of Higher Education," someone called it. It had 100,000 students, 50,000 faculty, 50,000 staff (as I recall). How would I like being a part of this? Size is a comparative term. To those who had experienced its rapid growth, it seemed to have become huge. Compared with State government, where I had been, it seemed smaller, more manageable, less bureaucratic.

Its structure might very well make it difficult to get things done – in fact, one purpose of university structure is to resist sudden change and to prevent central control. The Board of Regents was a prestigious group of mostly corporate-type achievers. The campuses were semi-autonomous fiefdoms where skillful chancellors survived by protecting the faculty, negotiating with the students, flattering the alumni and keeping the staff in line. The President of the University presided over the campus confederation, focusing on keeping the Regents and the State satisfied, the alumni and public supportive, and the funding generous. Where in the midst of all this was there a role for a middle manager concerned with administrative services – a person neither a part of the top leadership not a part of the grass-root operations, but floating somewhere between in a sort of central staff limbo? I felt that I could handle it, with the help of my experience elsewhere and of the excellent Vice-President who would be my immediate boss.

I did also see clearly that the University did not have a concept of management, unlike either the private sector (business administration) or the public sector (public administration). The basic administrative principle was a self-governing faculty whose academic freedom was protected against both internal and external interference. In its traditional scheme of professors, academic administrators, students, and clerks, the term "manager" or "executive" does not fit. Could one manage without authority or status? I looked forward to a collegial role and to earning acceptance from the academic community.

I did ask for the same salary I had been receiving in Sacramento (including my part-time teaching pay). It would be an expensive move (I was paying my own expenses), I would no longer be teaching, and I could not afford to take a salary cut. Also, I must admit, I wanted to be sure the University valued me and valued the position enough to pay what I was worth. At this point, there was a sudden long, silent pause, during which I just about decided to forget the whole thing.

A long time later, I learned what had been happening inside the University: an internal impasse over salary. My sponsors sought approval for the salary and the appointment. Apparently, some academic administrators could not conceive of paying a non-academic person (with no doctorate) that high a salary just to handle some routine housekeeping chores. Eventually, the approval was reluctantly given — but more out of political urgency than out of high regard for the work.

The University felt that some of its administrative services might be vulnerable to attack by the new Reagan administration and apparently decided that I could assist in handling the problem. It also helped that one of my sponsors in the University was chosen to become the new President of the University, moving from acting President to President. (Governor Reagan had played a prominent part in the sudden firing of the previous university president, an action which was widely seen as showing the willingness of the Reagan administration to intervene in university affairs.)

There are two parts to making a transition: the leaving and the arriving. I handled the second better than the first.

In leaving, everything was smooth and proper on the surface. I left with proper notice, in proper steps and with proper relations, but without much regret on either side. A heartening number of friends and associates did wish me well — with some private expressions of a certain envy at my escape to greener pastures. Nevertheless, in the language of bureaucracy the only two really acceptable ways to leave an organization are to retire or die.

What I was doing was by choice — a voluntary departure, which is seen by some as a kind of willful rejection of the old group. There is a certain bureaucratic resentment that one has chosen to "jump ship." Also, as soon as word goes out, some people begin immediately to think about the organization (and the possible new opportunities) without you. Organizations have very short memories, particularly when there has just been a traumatic change of direction at the top. In a short time people begin to be more surprised that you are still there than that you are leaving (this is not necessarily personal, just the way it often works).

It is usually possible, however, to retain at least a few work friendships after you leave – but it takes work. I think I could have handled this better. I gave the new organization my full attention and loyalty and did not spend much time renewing old connections. In Berkeley, I did not want to bring along the baggage of a Sacramento bureaucrat. In Sacramento, people were focused on their new situations as well. We rapidly "lost touch."

I think now that some of this could have been overcome if I had made those connections and friendships a higher priority. I tend to focus mostly on the present and the future, but there was in this departure a real sense of loss after twenty years. It was painful to go back. I admire those who have a talent for the quick, casual, frequent, thoughtful, spontaneous contacts which keeps friendships alive over distance. Maybe I considered my work friendships too much as having been functional. Maybe I should have valued their intrinsic pleasure more highly. The few friendships that did last seemed all the more satisfying.

As for the arrival in the new organization, there seem to me to be some useful general guidelines.

1. Extend the arrival period. Usually you are entitled to a sort of "honeymoon" period in which to get acquainted and learn the job. You are judged more leniently during this time, and will be expected to need more help. Use the newcomer role, even if it means exaggerating a bit the extent of the help you need. Unless there is a crisis, take more time.

2. Keep your options open. When you arrive, some people will immediately want to help you see your role as they do. Use the help, but keep your sources open and varied. Do a lot of walking around. Be in touch with as many people as you can.

It is particularly useful to talk with people who may well not be on your side. Seek them out; now is a particularly good time to hear what they are saying – before their criticisms become directed at you, and before you need to defend yourself to them. Don't overlook people outside the organization, too – clients, customers, suppliers, etc. – who may have very different views.

3. Accept the situation initially as you find it. It may be tempting to display your competence by telling how you used to do it somewhere else or by being quick to point out weaknesses and problems. Resist the temptation. Your first need is to understand things as they are. Analysis and change should usually be a later step.

4. Establish a basis for trust. Even as you sustain the "new arrival" role, you need to find out what various people expect of you and begin to respond to those expectations as positively as you can. Assume initially that people are capable and trustworthy and act accordingly toward them. Do not make sudden, unexplained changes, especially if they are adverse to people whose cooperation you need.

5. Watch out for set-ups and other tests. Once in a while, there may be early attempts to see how you react or to involve you in difficult decisions. Watch out for sudden proposals to change authority or policy or to disapprove fairly routine transactions, particularly when these show up on your desk with little consultation or preparation. Again, you can use your newcomer status (and your common sense). Avoid being drawn into premature or contrived issues for which you are unprepared.

6. Do your homework. As a newcomer, one of your problems is all the background and history you do not know. The files can be a rich source, particularly as a cross-check or a supplement to what you are told. It takes time to research such material (minutes, policies, major studies and reports, news releases, laws, manuals, etc.). Since your time is limited, don't try to research everything at once. Be guided by your sense of your current needs. If you can, let staff people do as much of this for you as possible.

7. Have a strategy for the first six months or more, but keep on changing it and refining it as things happen. Without some such plan, you are likely to be controlled by events, responding haphazardly to day-by-day details or to the initiatives of various other people. Without some planning, it is easy to overlook important moves you should be making. Your initial planning, however, is likely to be flawed because of all you don't know at the time, so expect it to be merely a first draft. Accept the fact, too, that at least half of your work will come from the plans of others and from unexpected events. Expect the unexpected and allow for it.

8. Do not hesitate to be yourself and to respond naturally. Despite the need for initial caution and careful planning, remember that people need to get to know you, and vice versa. What you need is not some controlled image or neutral personality. Follow your instincts, particularly in meetings, phone calls, memos, socializing, site visits, and other informal contacts. People need to know you as a real person and initially this is probably more important than your official actions.

9. Seek feedback on how you are doing. This means not just saying you are open to it but actively seeking it. When you get feedback, really pay attention to it. Do not use it as a basis for quick rebuttal. Whether it is right or wrong (as you see it), feedback is useful. Give information in order to get information – it needs to be a two-way exchange.

Do not overlook the special kind of feedback which can come from someone who is interested in your situation but outside the organization (a spouse or good friend, for example). Try telling such a person how you think you are doing. Describe incidents or problems and how you are handling them.

Even without first-hand knowledge, a sympathetic and sensitive listener can do several helpful things: (1) ask questions, the answers to which may help you see situations more clearly; (2) give you reactions, which may help you understand the interpersonal aspects of what is happening; (3) allow you to talk freely about your work, a process in which you may discover new facets and surface overlooked possibilities. (This is not therapy, just shop talk in a particularly safe and supportive setting – office gossip, if you will.) It will help you make sense of your work life.

10. Learn to communicate in the language of the organization. Every organization has its special identity and its preferred ways of communicating. When entering a new organization, it is wise to pay attention to these – "insider" jargon, organizational etiquette, personal styles, implied beliefs and values. The way you communicate may be "correct" general usage, but less appropriate or effective in a particular organization. You do not need to remake yourself, but some awareness may suggest simple adjustments.

For example, civil service organizations tend to use impersonal, rational language and style. Persuasion in such organizations often uses laws, rules, fairness, equal treatment, reason, and a sense of the public interest. There is an implication that the laws and the organization are more important than individuals.

In a university, however, it is academic intellect and personal style which is most admired. Persuasion often uses a large vocabulary, sophisticated analysis, assumes special knowledge, makes careful distinctions. There is an implication of individual intellect in pursuit of truth.

In government, rank relates to the hierarchy. In universities, rank relates to the academic discipline and tenure. In government, the official executive manner is often somewhat grey, deliberately neutral-sounding, undistinctive and impersonal, as if to say "I am merely a public servant doing my job." In a university, the official manner is often somewhat more individual, given to well-turned phrases, deliberate speech, thorough presentation, quiet charisma and poise, as if to say "I am a professor who happens to be doing this administrative chore."

> If all this seems too large a stretch or too boring or too artificial, take comfort in the fact that many large organizations also accommodate a limited number of officials who do not fit the prevailing mold. If you are able to demonstrate more than the usual competence or commitment or understanding, you may be allowed (even encouraged) to be yourself – even a self which is a bit different (but not too different).

When does the transition period end? It all depends. I would say it ends successfully at about the time you are no longer being introduced as the "new" whatever-you-are. For the organization, you are now a regular. There is, however, a more personal end to the transition, as well: it is when you discover yourself thinking of the organization you left as "they" and your new organization as "we." However long or short a time it takes, when these two things happen your transition period is probably over.

Chapter Fifteen

PROGRAMS

THE USUAL WAYS in which managers think about operations – in terms of the organization and the functions and the procedures and the resources – are very useful for some purposes, but lack a unifying focus: what is the purpose? Recasting these elements into a program can be a powerful management tool.

When I arrived at University Hall (the Berkeley headquarters for the statewide nine-campus system) I learned that my first priority should be to improve University purchasing. Rather than merely make improvements in various purchasing activities, I decided the situation called for a major new program: the Planned Purchasing Program. It is a good illustration of the usefulness and effectiveness of the concept of program management.

Before I arrived, the University had surveyed prices being paid at campuses for a sampling of common items. Each campus did its own purchasing, so it was not surprising that the prices varied widely. The staff report concluded that if all campuses were to purchase at the lowest prices of any, millions might be saved.

The Reagan administration was organizing task forces to look for waste in government operations. The purchasing system for State government was highly centralized. If University purchasing was seen as inefficient, the University could lose its valued independence in purchasing, and in other administrative services as well.

On the other hand, the University was deeply committed to decentralization in most academic and administrative affairs. Some officials reacted initially by blaming the survey for creating the problem – a reaction which seemed both unfair and unwise. Others felt it was urgent to take corrective action.

There was plenty of potential for conflict over this issue. The conventional wisdom among government purchasing professional specialists (including the excellent ones on my staff at the University) was to centralize control of all purchasing, buy all the big-ticket and quantity items centrally, let the operating units make some small purchases, and monitor their compliance.

To the campuses, "central" meant central campus purchasing, not central University-wide purchasing. Campus purchasing officers wanted to control purchasing centrally at the campus, handle the major items directly, let the departments buy only lesser items. The role of the systemwide office had been to establish systemwide policies and to handle a few big purchases (automobiles, etc.). In purchasing, as in most other administrative services, the campuses looked for authority to the campus chancellor, not to the systemwide staff.

The most important part of this administrative triangle was neither the systemwide nor the campuswide managers; it was the faculty. There might be differences over the proper central or campus role, but administrators at least had in common a belief in the usefulness of administrative services. To many faculty members, such activities were at best nuisances and at worst threats to academic freedom.

In purchasing for example, standardizing commodities for quantity purchase at lower prices might prevent academic researchers and their staffs from specifying their exact needs and would probably increase the time required to make purchases. Some faculty could provide anecdotes – rather lovingly collected, in fact, and widely circulated – of dumb staff decisions and bureaucratic bumbles. From this viewpoint, any increase in central control of "services" looked like interference – a thing to be opposed and, if necessary, subverted.

More basically, if a conflict was seen as academic freedom vs. administrative bureaucracy, the University had long since (and correctly) chosen academic freedom. In those terms, the less administration the better. As the University expanded, the growth of administrative services may have seemed to some like letting more and more barbarians within the academic walls.

This brief background (somewhat cartoonish) about the situation may help explain what followed: the development of a program which would do what needed to be done quickly and with as wide support as possible.

It seemed to me that the essential elements were these:

- Steps should be taken to make the University less vulnerable to criticism of its purchasing practices and costs.

- These steps should not conflict with basic academic values or campus authority.

- The changes should be made quickly and with the support of campus chancellors and purchasing staffs.

- To these were added (in collaboration with the central purchasing office) some further elements:

The University is not going to establish or fund a large central purchasing office.

- Campus purchasing officers have a lot in common as purchasing professionals and could work together much more if there were a system which encouraged it.

- Campus chancellors would not mind such inter-campus cooperation if it did not affect their authority.

- Faculty fears, while exaggerated, are real and must be respected. Any changes need to have safeguards and benefits which respond to the concerns of faculty (and of their staffs).

- There must be an honest and timely system for tracking the results of changes. Claimed savings and benefits must be verifiable and trustworthy.

- The changes must offer some incentives and some benefits for users besides lower prices – faster service, more flexibility, more participation.

At this point, it seemed obvious that it would take an array of related and detailed changes to move the purchasing system. Many constituencies would be involved. The changes needed to be packaged into a program. The program as a whole would be more visible and acceptable, more understandable, more significant than if its parts were undertaken as mere changes in procedure and policy.

As a program, the proposed changes could be circulated widely in draft to campus and systemwide officials, for discussion, comments and revisions. We needed not merely the attention and participation of purchasing officers and their staffs, but of campus chancellors and other leaders. A program has a name, an identity, an impact which justifies this kind of widespread attention. It also makes it easier to see the need for balance among its various elements.

The University's Planned Purchasing Program emerged from this process, a two or three page action plan:

1. Each campus purchasing office is to devote at least 10% of its professional staff time to developing University-wide purchasing contracts for a group of commodities.

2. Contracts will be based on projections of system-wide requirements for all campuses and will provide prices and terms for deliveries to each campus on demand during the contract period.

3. Inter-campus committees, representing a variety of users and campuses, will develop requirements for each major commodity group, exchange information, and participate in purchasing decisions, working with the appropriate campus purchasing officer.

4. After contracts are let, campus users will be able to order deliveries directly from contract vendors without going through the campus purchasing offices. Purchasing offices will help with problems, if needed, and will approve purchases outside the contract as necessary.

5. The University-wide staff will work with campuses to establish the system of campus commodity assignments, to develop procedures and policies, to provide coordination, to

> maintain liaison with the State and other public purchasing agencies, to monitor and compile reports of program results. The University-wide staff will arrange for University use of State purchasing contracts when appropriate.

How did it work out? The campus chancellors gave the program their approval and support, and it was approved by the University President, all much faster than I had thought possible. (It is worth noting that an implicit threat of outside investigation can be a powerful motivator for prompt action – another aspect of the usefulness of management by conflict and controversy. Sometimes the mere possibility of outside attack is enough.)

The Planned Purchasing Program did save the University millions during the next few years. The inter-dependent system, where each campus purchased some things for all the other campuses and in turn relied on other campuses for some purchasing, fostered healthy interactions and mutual interests. Central leadership became a help, not a threat. The system was neither centralized nor decentralized but a mixture of both.

Within a few years, the University was able to show that the prices it paid for many major purchases were at or below those obtained by the State operation and by other major public and private purchasing offices. A Reagan private industry task force did visit the University, but University purchasing did not become an issue.

There were problems, of course. No program works entirely as intended. The most difficult problem was to keep the campuses motivated to put in the necessary 10% of their time on system-wide purchasing. The pressure for service from local campus clients was sometimes more urgent than the needs of unseen customers at other campuses. However, because all campuses wanted a more-or-less equal time and effort from others, in return for their own efforts, the matter tended eventually to be self-correcting.

Constituting it as a program and disseminating widely the periodic reports of results also helped to keep up the momentum. In the early years, the excitement of the new program and the satisfaction of good results also helped. The potential of the program was so great that even less than ideal implementation was good enough.

We could afford to tolerate a lot of leakage in the new system and still feel it was a big improvement.

I always had a friendly difference of opinion with the purchasing specialists about one aspect of the program. They were enthusiastic supporters of the Planned Purchasing Program and proud of its results. They saw the program, however, as a compromise – a matter of settling for less than the best purchasing practices in the face of practical limitations. They still hoped that it was a step on the way toward a fully centralized purchasing system.

On the other hand, I always regarded the program as the best system for the whole University, all things considered – not a compromise but an integration of complex and varied interests. Many specialists, I suppose, honestly prefer a simple system which gives their special skills and interests free rein. Most specialists probably operate under something less than what they would consider ideal conditions – and rightly so. They deal in means, not ends. They should serve the needs of the University, not vice versa.

As a generalist manager, I feel that the best balance is usually less than ideal for any constituency, but one which meets the real needs of all. It is incorrect to call this compromise (the word suggests settling for less in the face of resistance and conflict). Mary Follette, a wise and pioneering management consultant, used the term "creative integration," by which she meant a solution which met the real needs of all parties and worked within the limits of the situation, often in a new and distinctive way (in the more current language, a win-win solution).

I believe that management programs which focus on your most important goals do help encourage unified and integrated approaches. You are more likely to deal with all the elements of the situation and to consider the less obvious relationships. Specialists are forced to adjust to broader values. It is easier for people to accept a program than a series of apparently unrelated changes. It increases the visibility and importance of particular activities. They help keep attention fixed on basics despite the distractions of day-by-day routines and happenings. Programs can remind you of what a manager most needs to know: what you are trying to do – and how it can be done.

Chapter Sixteen

RELATIONSHIPS

WE NEED TO talk about the importance to managers of relationships, about the variety of people in work organizations, and about diversity.

Many managers think of themselves as able to relate to many different sorts of people, and think of their organizations as diverse. In fact, it is common for managers to hire people whom they know or whom they know about — people who are often very like themselves. They exaggerate small differences in appearance or dress or manner, as if these showed real diversity. It is sometimes difficult for managers to realize the range of diversity which is not represented at all.

Another tendency is to look to a few individuals as tokens of diversity. ("Do you have women executives?" "Oh, yes, we have one!" or "Do you hire minorities?" "Oh, yes, we have several!") Such exceptions are seen as symbolizing a diversity which is in fact very limited.

Managers like to emphasize unity. So many things in organizations are standardized. It may be easy to accept the idea that people also need in some way to be standardized, and to think of the common qualities of those we already know as requirements, whether they really are or not.

Oddly, managers are perhaps over-willing to accept one kind of diversity: job specialists. Organizations are full of people defined by education and training as one kind of specialist or another. When it comes to occupational specialties and qualifications, we accept and even demand a diversity of advance requirements which can be excessive. We do not so much hire people as their labels, their credentials.

The attitude is often quite different toward other kinds of diversity: gender, race, age, culture, lifestyle, sexual orientation. The diversity of specialists is seen as a necessary fact of modern life;

other kinds of diversity are more likely to be seen as threats or as externally imposed requirements.

Over the years of my experience, however, I think that many managers (including me) have become much more aware of the need for diversity — of being open to the many who have felt excluded or unaccepted or mistreated. Legal requirements have changed, but so (in many cases) has management thinking.

Diversity in work organizations is important not only as a matter of public policy and social justice, but as a matter of good management. Although the traditional language of management is impersonal and abstract, the real core of management is personal relationships — concepts of leadership, motivation, communication, coordination, cooperation, etc. become real only in the interactions of people with one another. Managers need to be able to relate effectively with a much wider range of diversity than they encountered in the past.

Three points I would like to emphasize from my own experience with regard to diversity:

1. Diversity (differences) is as necessary and valuable in organizations as unity (community). These are not incompatible. Organizations need both.

2. Diverse work groups need to perform at common levels of quality. To expect less of the "new" people is simply bias in a subtler form. As the workforce becomes more diverse, the kind of development and guidance needed may become more varied, but the expectation of full performance has to extend across the board.

3. The most challenging aspect for managers of diverse organizations may be the understanding of cultural differences. Every manager knows that you cannot treat everybody alike. Everyone relates to different people in somewhat different ways. However, as cultural differences become wider and more varied, it becomes more complicated.

My work group at the University was more varied than in State government – probably a result of different location, different personnel practices, and the passage of time. Mostly, the learning experiences and the relationships were enjoyable. However, I had a sad and humbling experience in understanding cultural differences, so I will use that experience as an example.

One of the most promising and personable individuals in the office was a bright and talented young man from Southeast Asia, who was developing a University-wide system of telephone communications to serve the campuses.

Forced to leave his own country by political turmoil, he and his wife had come to California. There he had established himself in the telephone industry (both technically and personally) in a rather short time. He had then come to the University as a further advancement.

It did not occur to me to think of cultural differences. Even though he and his wife had been through much trauma and disruption, they seemed to me to have adapted successfully and completely to American ways. Nobody at work was more enthusiastic and energetic and committed. His wife was active and talented in volunteer work teaching art to children in San Francisco. He took special pride in his Thunderbird sports car.

I did feel a cultural difference, a formality, an etiquette of respect toward age and authority, which was different but not unpleasant. My wife and I enjoyed wonderful foods of their native country when entertained at their home. Their charming little boy was obviously much loved. They seemed a very happy young family.

After a couple of years, however, things seemed to change. He became withdrawn and moody at work, and began to close his office door most of the time. He still did outstanding work, but somehow the enthusiasm seemed to have become a bit forced.

My usual approach was not to inquire into personal matters unless they affected the work or the person brought them up in conversation. There had been some comments to me from other staff members and I felt some personal concern for him.

With some staff, I would have felt freer to inquire. With others, I might still have held back. In this case, without too much thought, I simply asked him directly one day what was happening (we were going to Sacramento in his sports car, and it seemed a convenient time). I did not think whether an inquiry from his boss might carry special impact or put him under pressure. I just wanted to know, so I asked.

He immediately explained that in recent months he had been having personal problems which had affected him at work. He said that he and his wife had been separated, that she and their son had been in Southern California. However, he said that those problems had just been solved – that they were reuniting, that his wife and child would soon be back with him in Berkeley, that everything was just fine again. He sounded so cheerful and confident (his old self again) that I just expressed pleasure, thanked him for telling me, and somewhat put it out of my mind.

A few days later the police called me at the office and I learned the shocking truth. There had been no reunion. Their son had been visiting him and was to return to his mother that day. The father had shot and killed the little boy. He had then shot and killed himself. A note explained that he was making sure he and his son would always be together.

In one sense, all this had little to do with me. I mourned a colleague and his child and sympathized with his widow. I can only say, however, that as a manager I felt a strong sense of failure. Whether I had intervened too late or too soon, too much or too little, too casually or too awkwardly – I felt completely unsure.

I had thought I understood the situation. I had thought I could just treat him like any other hard-working young colleague. I knew his deference to superiors, his anxiety to please, his pride. My direct inquiry had probably added considerably to the pressures on him, rather than helping. Somehow, I should have understood him better as a person – or should have realized I did not understand enough.

It was a dramatic example of a more general lesson in management: to know people primarily through work is usually to know them only in a limited way. We need to understand one another insofar as it affects the work, but managers have no special right to invade personal privacy and no inherent ability to play therapist. When differences of rank and status are involved, what managers intend as a helpful friendly interest in personal matters may be received as pressure and probing.

Given such limitations, what can managers do to develop and maintain positive work relationships? After all, things get done a lot more often because people get together and cooperate than because orders are given and received.

The first thing to get in mind, I think, is that people do not need to be like you in order for you to work well together. The best boss I ever had was very different from me in many ways. However, we had a mutual appreciation of the differences. Some of the differences between us complemented one another. Others just didn't seem important in our working together. I was clearly the subordinate, but I never felt subordinated.

Which brings up the inadequacy of our terminology for the relationships of command and responsibility in organizations. Boss connotes work slavery. Superior suggests inferior. Supervisor is good, but usage limits it to the heads of small groups. Leader is better – the complement is follower, which is part of the picture, too. Our language of organizations still shows its roots in the military. Perhaps we just have to let time modify and broaden the meanings of the old words.

I like the terms manager and management and use them more often than other labels. The terms apparently have their root in two old French words which originally meant the management of horses (a special way of training them to perform) and the menagement of a large household (having charge of the ménage). Training and service – not a bad combination.

Administrator and administration are good words too – ministering to the needs of the organization puts the emphasis in a different place. Executive? OK, I guess, as a noun – probably the most popular term now for a business leader. But as a verb – to execute – well, you see the problem.

Back to personal relationships. Organizations often set up certain relationship rules (often unwritten, but customary) and so do managers. If your manager holds staff meetings, then those staff meetings are important (use them well). If certain channels of contact are expected, use them (and make them work for you). Do certain people expect certain courtesies and deference? Do it (but don't make it a big thing, either). Are presentations to groups considered important? Learn to do them well.

In other words, some of your personal relationships are prescribed by the organization. Beyond these, you usually have a good deal of latitude. Think of personal relationships not just as something which "happens" between people in organizations, but as something which is worth your continued thought and care.

The more diverse the organization, the more important it is to focus in on developing and maintaining personal relationships. They are the glue which holds work organizations together (structure tends to split them apart). Pay attention to personal relationships. If they are not going well, pay particular attention – it is an important sign. If they are going well, you can feel it – and it feels good.

Chapter Seventeen

ACTING MANAGER

THE ACTING OR interim manager is a special role which has its own distinctive opportunities and problems. Although not much discussed in the literature, the concept is becoming more widely recognized in organizations, such as universities (and churches), which take a very long time to recruit executive replacements. There is more turnover these days in such organizations, and a greater need for acting managers who fill the leadership gap between "regular" appointments.

I spent a year as Acting Vice President, Business and Finance, at the University of California, and experienced some of both the opportunities and the problems. It happened unexpectedly and I was unprepared. It might have helped to have some better idea of how to enter, to perform, and to exit such a temporary assignment.

The Vice President died of a heart attack, suddenly, over a weekend. The next day, the President asked me to look after things until a replacement could be appointed. It was an informal request, and I more or less automatically agreed. There was no added pay, no new appointment, no indication of a length of time. I would keep on doing my regular job plus the extra work. It did not seem to me a step toward the Vice-Presidency, which I knew was likely to go to someone with a prestigious academic or business career.

It might have been better if matters had been dealt with a little more clearly at the start. As it was, I started out assuming it would be a brief, minimum caretaker task, and gradually slid into the full Vice-President role through the pressure of events and the passage of time. The assignment developed in small pragmatic steps without further discussion with the President. It just seemed that what had to be done kept increasing, and he seemed satisfied to have me do it.

In this somewhat ambiguous situation, I moved with some caution. I went to meetings of Vice-Presidents only after checking whether I was expected. I asked for delegations of authority only as the need arose. I continued to work in my own office and went to the Vice-President's office only as needed there. I led staff meetings with a particularly low-key collegial style.

On the other hand, organizations make work for executives. The flow of communications, processes, schedules, and decisions is inexorable. After the initial shock wears off, people in the organization feel a strong need for the wheels to start turning again.

I had little individual contact with the President, except in group meetings. Vice-Presidents normally have a great deal of latitude to manage without checking with the President, and in this interim the President seemed to prefer even less contact.

In the systemwide office, the monthly meetings of the governing board, the Board of Regents, are a major fact of work life. I had made presentations to the Board before, and was used to the elaborate rituals by which written material was prepared and approved for Board agendas. (I had once written a deadpan imitation Regent's item for an office Christmas party in the form of a policy authorizing employees to send Christmas cards.)

It now became necessary to communicate informally with Regents who were Finance Committee or Audit Committee members. The full Board took the actions, but the meetings of the Finance and Audit committees were usually the decisive forum for the matters which I was handling. Even though I kept these contacts informal and low-key, they were still necessary and they did involve me in a different kind of relationship.

Gradually, I developed my own goals. What I most wanted was to see whether I could do the job of a Vice-President and do it well enough to satisfy myself. The strengths of my situation (and probably of many interim situations) were that (1) most people would want me to do well, (2) certain long-range problems and initiatives were better left to the permanent replacement, and (3) the detailed knowledge I already had of the University meant that I could get some things done faster and easier than a newcomer.

After several months, in which the replacement process appeared to extend more and more into the future, I felt confident that things were going well. I was appointed officially as acting Vice President. Although still realistic in expecting a prestigious outside appointment would eventually be made, I decided to apply for the job myself. If the search was taking this long, it must be somewhat of an open situation, and I felt my performance as acting Vice President might carry some special weight. I wanted to let the President know that I was interested and would accept the job if it was offered, even though he had not asked.

For me, the problem of being both acting temporarily in the job and being an applicant for the permanent appointment became the most difficult aspect of my situation. When I applied, I did not foresee the mixed feelings it would arouse in me, which I was never able to resolve fully. On the one hand, I recognized that I did not fit the usual criteria for the appointment. On the other hand, as the months went by and the office was running very well and I was getting a lot of positive feedback, I felt in my own mind that I had some excellent qualifications.

I still kept mainly to the idea of satisfying myself rather than expecting any reward, but it was hard not to think "what if?" sometimes. What I also failed to anticipate was how much more difficult it would be to go back to my regular job having been a job contender. There is a lot of difference between (1) completing a temporary assignment and (2) being replaced in a job for which you have applied. It feels different to you, it looks different to other people in the organization, and it may seem different to your permanent replacement, a person with whom you will be working.

After six months in the acting assignment, I did another thing that made a kind of statement. I had applied for the job. I was doing what had grown to two full-time management jobs. The office was in good shape. The campuses were happy. I was tired. I had decided that if matters were not resolved by the sixth-month point I would designate one of my peers as acting (acting-acting, really) and take off on a much-needed one-month vacation It was the time when University vice-presidents vacationed – so I went, to Europe. I wanted to be where people could not easily contact or summon me. My wife and I had a great month-long vacation. The office got along fine without me, and I got along fine without it.

This vacation felt like a kind of declaration to me: "I insist on doing the job my way; I'll do the temporary appointment; I'd like to keep on being the Vice-President, but if it happens it happens on my terms." If good performance was the criterion, I felt that I had shown it. If something else was required, then no, thanks. I was not staying there to knock myself out while everyone else vacationed. That's what it felt like to me, anyway; whether anyone else got the message, I do not know.

After nearly a year, the President appointed a candidate with a long and distinguished career in government and business and higher education. I was genuinely enthusiastic at the prospect of working for him. He would handle a broader range of responsibilities than the previous Vice-President had. I was promoted to Assistant Vice President to handle both my old job and to be an aide to the new Vice President. It seemed to me a good solution.

Nevertheless, the next few months were in some ways bumpy. It is surprisingly difficult to adjust to a lesser role in the same organization – like an understudy, perhaps, who is applauded for stepping into a leading role and then goes back to a supporting part. Organizations are not constituted to offer much positive support to those who move to a lesser role. It seems too much like a demotion. People in organizations live in the present, not the past. They support those who seem on the way up, not down.

What issues does this example raise about the role of the Acting Manager?

1. Think before you apply or accept. (Think not just of the present but of the future.)

2. Be clear about what you are to do and whether or not you seek the permanent job. (If these aren't clear, clarify them – and soon.)

3. Be particularly careful of the transitions – moving in and moving out of the interim job. (Pay attention to your own feelings, as well as being sensitive to those of others.)

4. Make it look easy, if you can. (It is often a time for reassurance and stability and healing.)

5. Do not become too attached to the role. (No matter how long it lasts, you need to be prepared to let go.)

6. If you plan to stay on in a former position, plan for that with particular care. (Your return may not be easy for your staff who kept things going while you were away. Your continued presence may not be entirely welcome to the new manager, who has succeeded you.)

7. Be realistic about the situation. (This probably means focusing on the achievable, enjoying the experience and the learning, and expecting mainly self-satisfaction.)

I wish more people would try a sort of variation on the Acting Manager concept: the Virtual Acting Manager. I have used the device often, but until recently never had a good term for it. You probably will never be asked be an Acting Manager. What you can do many times is put yourself mentally in the role of a specific manager – perhaps your boss, perhaps your boss's boss. Think specifically what you would do if you had this job? Look at issues, at people, at yourself through the eyes of that manager, with as much reality as possible.

Virtual managing is an excellent way to change your viewpoint, to gain empathy, to broaden your understanding, to prepare for being a manager or for advancement in management. If you are in the habit of putting yourself in the role of a manager, you will be more ready if an opportunity comes to assume a management post. At the very least, you will have the experience of knowing that your understanding of management and managers is improving.

One other postscript: as acting Vice-President I had, as already mentioned, my closest working with a governing board the Board of Regents. For managers, the relationship often involves a paradox: a governing board should be the highest level of leadership and responsibility, yet for a manager the best board is one which merely approves everything the executive proposes. How can a body be both the ultimate power and a rubber stamp?

Board-watching and the care and feeding of board members becomes a survival skill for executives who report to them. Things are not always as they seem. Boards and executives recognize the need for a certain appearance of give-and-take. Of course, to actually disapprove a major proposal may signal a crisis of confidence in the executive. It is not always easy to read the signals, nor are all the members necessarily sending the same signals.

Part of the executive skill is in judging just how much information board members can handle – enough for them to feel they are ready to vote approval, but not enough for them to become confused or upset by too much complexity. Some board members like to make a point in a meeting, whether it has any lasting impact or not. Others want to have an impact, whether it shows in a board meeting or not (and often it does not). Managers need to read and respond to the board as a whole and to the individual members as well.

It is in times of crisis (which can arise suddenly and unexpectedly) that the true importance of boards shows. The rest of the time, their main power may be invisible: proposals are not made to the board at all because of a sense that they would not be approved – at least not at the time. Board meetings give us the unusual opportunity of seeing managers in the unaccustomed role of subordinate, but all things considered it is likely (most of the time) to be the board which is being managed.

I have always enjoyed being a board watcher (and a legislature watcher and a committee watcher). They provide such fascinating performances, sometimes rehearsed and sometimes improvised. No matter how carefully planned, board meeting may always go unexpectedly out of control or off in some unforeseen direction. There are simply too many players and too many relationships ever to be sure what will happen.

Case in point: the Board of Regents and Governor Reagan. The Governor had always been a member ex officio of the Board, but before Reagan the actual participation had been limited to ceremonial occasions and times of crisis. Reagan blandly started showing up at nearly every meeting as soon as he took office, startling everyone and changing the whole dynamics in unexpected ways.

He did not attend committees, but on Fridays, when the full Board and the media were present, he was there. Most of the time, he was rather quiet. Once in a while he would have a statement to make. It was usually a statement, not a discussion, and he seemed well-prepared. Although everyone was intensely conscious of his presence, he often sat through meetings with seemingly little impact.

When the meeting adjourned, the press conference started. Technically, the President and the Governor both appeared, but usually the Governor immediately captured and held the media spotlight as well as the TV cameras. He always attended meetings in full makeup and was ready to look his best on camera. Often he had a newsy prepared statement. The topic might target the University, but often the Governor's topic was something else, which took the headlines instead of the Regents meeting. Often, from reading the papers or watching the TV news, you would have had a completely different impression of both the Board of Regents and the Governor.

My impression of the Governor on these occasions was not the same as the conventional wisdom. His smile was familiar, but in person he seemed to me not particularly affable. He was sometimes quite caustic and demanding, but more often just vaguely bored. It was at the news conference that he came alive – this was clearly the real event. He knew exactly where his real audience was, and usually it was not the small crowd at a Regent's meeting. Even though I could see the tactics and the technique, I had to admire the effectiveness with which it was done.

The Governor was not the only interesting Regent to watch. Catherine Hearst was chair of the Audit Committee; she stopped attending meetings when her daughter, Patricia, was kidnapped. Richard Haldemann, later one of Nixon's two chief White House aides, was at the time a Regent as head of the UC Alumni association; he looked like a crew-cut Marine. (I should have noticed him more). Norton Simon, rich and arrogant, sometimes took off on unexpected personal crusades of his own. William Roth, scion of the Dollar Lines and developer of San Francisco's innovative Ghirardelli Square, briefly campaigned for the Democratic nomination for Governor. Dorothy Chandler, of the Los Angeles Times Chandlers, was a long-time supporter of the University.

It was a group worth watching – not to mention the nine Chancellors of the University campuses, generally impressive and articulate, who were the leadership core of the University administration. My personal favorite among all the Regents, however, was Elinor Heller, a very effective member of the Board. She often asked extremely good questions, but her style (which I much appreciated) was to call you before the meeting and let you know what she was going to ask.

Chapter Eighteen

REASSIGNMENTS

REASSIGNMENT – MOVING a person from one job to another – can be a powerful management tool. If you are a manager, remember that matching people and assignments in a different way can be as useful as hiring new people. If you are offered a reassignment, consider it as carefully as if it were a job offer from another organization.

I was offered a reassignment about a year after I had become Assistant Vice President at the University. By this time, things seemed to be going well again. I was once more in charge of Business Services and had an excellent staff who looked after an interesting variety of services – purchasing, financing of self-supporting services (student housing, parking, etc.), insurance and risk management, telephone communications system, printing and copying, campus police.

In addition, I handled some special assignments for the Vice President, Business and Finance, which involved me in some of the more pressing problems of that office at his request. I had recovered from the trauma of my acting Vice-President experience and its aftermath. I felt comfortable and the situation looked more stable than usual. (In itself, my wife points out, a dangerous sign.)

Unexpectedly, the Vice President asked me to accept a reassignment to become Assistant Vice President and Controller. He proposed to demote the present Controller and to put me in his place. I would still handle special assignments for the Vice President. Someone else would replace me as head of Business Services.

I was so focused on doing whatever was asked of me and so programmed to welcome new experiences that I immediately said yes (even breaking my long-standing practice of talking it over with my wife before making a decision which involved us both). I asked only to take along a key assistant, with particular skills in financial analysis, and my secretary, and to be assured the present Controller would accept the changes. These conditions were met later that day.

I went back to my office with a curious sense that I had somehow been cut off at the knees, that I had said yes too fast, too uncritically, too confidently.

By this time, I had what I regarded as twenty-five years of successful administrative experience. I had moved from organization to organization and from situation to situation, always able to adapt and to meet the challenges. I forgot that we all have limits. Even a generalist like me can succeed only within a certain range of organizations and situations.

There was also an element of overtrust. I felt I had contributed a lot to University administration and that the University would in turn look after me. I had seen this happen with other people, but they were usually tenured academics or life-long University staff. I was still a relative newcomer. (I had also not lived through the infighting which marked earlier changes of Presidents, which had left some long-time staff with lasting scars and an excess of caution. I rejected these stories as not applicable – not now, not these days, not to me.)

I simply saw the Controller's job as another challenging opportunity. Earlier Controllers had been important in the development of the University. Accounting and finance were about the only areas of administration I had not worked in at one time or another. It also might open up a promotion, I thought, for one of my Business Services staff. The former Controller seemed very positive about our working together. When you have already said yes, it is remarkable how many positive reasons you can think of in support of your decision.

It is also remarkable how many negative aspects you can overlook, such as the following:

- I didn't really like accounting. (I can use it, but I don't really enjoy it.)

- I was not an accountant. (To accountants, whom I would be supervising, this is a serious limitation.)

- Having the former Controller as my deputy would be difficult. (If he had not succeeded before, why would he succeed now? How would the rest of our staff react to him?)

- I didn't know exactly how I would use the assistant I was bringing along. (What I knew was that he was capable and hardworking – but in what new job?)

- Did the University really want or need better accounting? (If the game is to spend all the available money before the authorization runs out, how sophisticated a system of management reporting do you need?)

If I had taken time and checked around more (as I usually had done) I might have learned some of the following as well:

- Moving me out of the Business Services position would open up an appointment for a long-time University staff attorney who might otherwise leave. (He had experience with business services in the military.)

- The University budget officer thought the position of Controller unnecessary. (A Chief Accountant would be enough, he believed.)

- The internal audit staff would not report to me, but directly to the Vice President, through a new Audit chief. (Instead of being an important tool for the Controller to monitor campus financial affairs, the audit became a check on both the campuses and the Controller's office.)

- The Controller would become responsible for collecting delinquent student loan payments through a central office. (The external auditors had recommended that it be centralized; campuses were glad to be relieved of what had become a very large problem.)

- The five rapidly growing University teaching hospitals were becoming a drain on the University's working capital. (Campuses looked to the systemwide office for a solution, but insisted on financial independence for the hospitals.)

- The Controller negotiated the overhead rates to be applied to Federal research grants to cover indirect costs. (The Federal government was tightening up its rules and its attitudes, jeopardizing a large flow of funds on which the University depended.)

- The Controller before the present one had resigned when criticized at a Regent's meeting for an unfavorable audit report. (He apparently felt that he had been made responsible for matters not under his control.)

Bottom line: I accepted this reassignment too easily.

Chapter Nineteen

CRISIS MANAGEMENT

B*OTH INDIVIDUALS AND* organizations can find themselves in crisis. Sometimes it is hard to separate one from the other. Is the problem in your self or your situation?

At the University, after nearly ten years, I was having some sort of crisis. I was finding little satisfaction in the job of Controller. Working as an aide to the Vice President seemed mostly a matter of too little and too late – I was involved too little to influence policies and too late to prevent problems. I was having some doubts about my own effectiveness as a manager.

Moreover, there was a new University President (always a nervous time for systemwide staff). This one was critical of the central office. One of his goals was to reduce central control and strengthen campus administration. Although I sympathized with his objective, I felt included in the new team's general suspicion of the central staff.

I contacted an aide close to the new President and told her that I would welcome an opportunity to help the new President. I said that I wanted to be a part of the new team and that I would be willing to take on some extra project. I asked her to keep me in mind.

Soon after – a few weeks, or a couple of months, at most – a sudden and severe crisis arose in the leadership of one of the newer campuses. The President was sending in an acting Chancellor – a long-time colleague, now one of his vice-presidents – and was forming a staff task force to help the acting Chancellor. I was asked (through my Vice President) to head the team. (Timely and appropriate, I thought – helping to manage a University crisis may help to manage my personal career crisis.)

The campus in crisis was one in which I had particular interest. I had worked with and admired the founding Chancellor, who had developed an innovative plan for residential colleges, each combining academic and student life in a distinctive way. He had brought the new campus, faculty, and student body to a point of considerable success before he retired. Our two older youngsters had graduated there. I was already very committed to helping the campus.

The crisis had become public when the faculty voted no confidence in the new Chancellor and took their grievances to the University President. The new Chancellor resigned. The campus was in an uproar. The President (with the approval of the Regents) appointed an Acting Chancellor to calm the crisis, restore confidence, and carry on until a permanent successor could be named (a process which could take up to a year).

The other members of the task force (also selected by the President) struck me as capable and of appropriately varied experience and skills. Each of us would be working at our regular campus or systemwide jobs while serving on the task force.

To me, it was a kind of management analysis assignment — a return to an earlier role, but with some important differences. It made me realize how much my own ideas of management and of consulting had changed.

It would be much more hands-on. We were still an outside team, in relation to the campus. Under the circumstances we needed to work in close support to the Acting Chancellor as a low-profile, trouble-shooting, flexible group — adding to his sources of information and responding to his leadership. At the same time, we needed to be looking at the longer-range situation, beyond the immediate crises. In both we needed to integrate our work fully with his.

The study process had to be different, too. We needed to see many people quickly in order to give a reassuring sense of our presence, to open communication lines, and to encourage people to express their feelings of anger, frustration, or dismay in a safe and private way.

While being widely visible, we also had to be sure that the spotlight was on the Acting Chancellor and not on us. He was a strong and effective leader in this crisis, and our own relatively modest role as a task force needed to remain in proper perspective for the campus. It was the Acting Chancellor and the results of his interim leadership which mattered. Everything we were doing was secondary to that.

We decided early on not to produce a final report – the traditional wrap-up publication of findings and recommendations. It did not fit the situation. Instead, we produced a series of brief memos which wrapped up specific topics and areas as we finished with them, summarizing what had already been done and documenting remaining proposals.

These reports were tools of the work in project. They were as varied as our task force membership and topics. We avoided compiling a massive report, but left a series of papers which in combination left an adequate trail.

Many of the findings and solutions came bubbling up from people at the campus, in rich variety and with considerable force. Many people felt strongly that they knew what had gone wrong and just wanted someone to listen to what they had to say. The shape of our proposals seemed to grow out of this process, more than from any independent analysis of our own.

The whole task force process took about six months. By that time, neither the Acting Chancellor nor the campus needed us any longer. Two of our task force members stayed on and joined the campus staff. (I came back later, in retirement, when a later Chancellor invited me back for another consulting assignment.)

The task force assignment invigorated me and renewed my self-confidence as a manager. Our approaches – the analytical low-key style, the interactions with the campus, the group process, the rapport with the Acting Chancellor, the prompt application of solutions, the informality – all had worked well and had contributed toward restoring a positive campus climate. It reassured me that my preference as a manager for a combination of analysis and collaboration and action was valid.

The experience strengthened my belief in an ancient Lao Tse proverb about good leadership: when the work was done the people on campus could say "we did it ourselves."

As for my own personal crisis – that too was resolved by the campus crisis-managing experience. The stimulation and satisfaction of the campus assignment made the negative aspects of the Controllership easier to bear – for a while. I felt very comfortable with the new President and his team and no longer had that sense of being under suspicion.

The most important result, however, was that I now saw that my personal career crisis resulted from my job situation and not from myself. I understood that in the right situation I could once again feel effective and satisfied. My wife and I quietly agreed that I would fire myself soon (by early retirement) and find something better to do. I realized that I could just walk away from the University and never look back.

PART FOUR

MANAGEMENT EDUCATION

Snapshot (1980)

IT WAS AGAIN a time of transition and change – change in family, in work life and in the way the world felt.

Marriage still great. Youngsters now young adults – more or less launched on their own separate lives, living elsewhere but still in touch. All three graduated from college. Two married. One grandchild. (At last, the joys of grandparenting!) Just the two of us at home now. More leisure, more travel, more free time.

Our parents and most of their peers were gone, the end of that era marked by the passing of my perennially vigorous ninetysomething aunt. Suddenly we were the older generation. I had retired from the University of California. It might have been a time for settling in, for coasting, for enjoying the years of (awful label) senior citizenship.

Instead, it was a time for starting out on a whole new career. I had not retired to become less active, but to find something better to do. It was a leap of faith, because I did not know what that something might be. With financial security, I had more freedom to choose for the satisfaction of the work itself. It was a time for recharging of batteries, for renewal, for doing some of the things we had intended to do "sometime."

An ad in a higher education publication had caught my eye: an innovative private university in nearby Orinda was looking for a Dean for its School of Management, heading a program of upper division and graduate education for mid-career working adults. It meant both teaching and managing, full-time, working with wonderful colleagues and dedicated students in a small and supportive organization. High on challenges, low on compensation – an ideal fit for me.

That I was sixtyish didn't matter, least of all to me. That I lacked a PhD seemed less important in this school than my years of experience as a manager and a teacher. In a place where most of the faculty were part-time teachers and full-time managers, I felt at home.

Pictures of this time? Betty and me in our little British sports car, touring California. Later, Betty and me, traveling in Europe during the academic breaks. Still later, Betty and me car-camping in our red pickup truck. Me at work: talking with prospective students, helping them sort out their goals; lively discussions in classrooms, making management come alive; handing out hard-earned degrees to students while their family support-groups cheered. Berkeley scenes: enjoying the view of Bay and bridges from our hillside deck; learning to use a personal computer for teaching – and, perhaps, for writing.

Chapter Twenty

MANAGEMENT TEACHER

THE COMBINATION OF teaching and practice makes sense in management, as it does in medicine and law and other professions. The teaching enriches the practice, the practice adds realism to the teaching.

During most of my years in State government, I had enjoyed teaching public administration students at Sacramento State University in the graduate program. The students were mostly State employees working for a Masters degree as part of their career plans – generally excellent students, purposeful, experienced, motivated and organized. It kept me learning.

While at the University of California, I had not taught. Faculty at a research university are generally required to have a PhD, and anyway the statewide travel to campuses left little time or energy for teaching. I tried it once at an evening program in San Francisco, but did not continue.

Over the years, my ideas of teaching had changed as much as my ideas of management. I remember preparing for my first course in public administration and worrying about how I could fill the hours. Did I have enough to tell them? I overprepared ridiculously to keep from running out of something to say. Unconsciously, I thought of it as a series of lectures, in which the material would go from my notes to their notes. Later on I would test to see how much they remembered. The students seemed like rows of containers, with open brains into which I would pour knowledge.

Fortunately, the Dean was a friend as well as an experienced teacher. He gave me some practical suggestions about the kind of active learning and participation which students, especially experienced adult students, prefer. From that base, plus years of trial and error, I built a teaching style which was more and more a matter of helping students take active responsibility for their learning, while I provided learning environment, process, and stimulus for the group.

The idea of pioneering an alternative model for management degree programs appealed strongly to me. Many universities at that time were still preoccupied with full-time students with little or no work experience. In management, which many discover or choose later, during their work careers, there was a particular need for quality part-time education. The idea of life-long learning (instead of stopping after the twenties) made sense in a changing work world. At traditional schools, many part-time students were at that time still being shunted off to non-degree "night school" classes. There were so many full-time baby-boomers that older part-timers were often refused admission to regular degree programs.

The conventional wisdom also limited the kind of faculty considered appropriate for degree programs. The force of academic accreditation and certification (and of academic prestige) was clearly behind full-time, doctoral faculty. University research was more prestigious than university teaching.

In a professional field, such as management, where students need to learn both theory and practice, it seemed to me that people who were primarily managers but who also taught part-time could provide an excellent alternative. They might need help with teaching methods for adult learners, but that could be true of faculty researchers as well, to whom a low teaching load was often a sign of prestige.

At John F. Kennedy University, the school where I was full-time Dean of Management, I developed further an approach to experiential learning in management. The experiential concept was not new. In general, it means using realistic material in the classroom – problems, cases, real-life experiences – as material for individual and group learning activities. Students learn to think like managers, to relate theory and practice, and to learn that there may be many appropriate courses of action in real management situations. Students in such a class are active participants, not passive listeners. The more mature and motivated they are, generally the better they like it.

The teacher using experiential methods becomes a kind of classroom leader, mentor or manager. In a management course, this adds another learning dimension. The teaching of management should be compatible with the ideas being taught. It seems inappropriate and disturbing to use top-down, authoritarian teaching to tell students that as real-life managers they should be group-oriented and participative leaders. The medium and the message need to reinforce one another.

Another disturbing aspect of much classroom teaching and learning is that it sets up a gap between learning and action. The learning cycle is self-contained: the student learns the material, perhaps even discusses it or writes papers about it or responds to questions about it. When tested on the material, the conscientious student will probably be able to show an understanding of the material and an ability to paraphrase the ideas.

What is disturbing is to find that this learning cycle may be almost entirely directed toward the passing of the course, and eventually the obtaining of the degree. There is often a large gap between this learning and an ability to apply the ideas in realistic situations. Asked to simulate or role play problems, to put the ideas into action, the gap is usually even larger.

For example, if you ask students to discuss some of the characteristics of an effective manager, or to read some material on the topic, a plausible list of qualities will quite readily be developed – usually one in which there are quite idealistic elements of leadership. Then give the students problem situations and ask them to propose appropriate managerial actions to solve them and you will often find the responses have little connection with the earlier abstractions. Worse, students do not even see the inconsistency between theory and action.

The explanation, I think, is that unless students are in some way helped to link the ideas of management and their own ideas and actions, the two may well remain unconnected. In my experience, the actions which are taken in case analyses or role-playing or management games are likely to be much more authoritarian, one-dimensional, arbitrary, and top-down traditional. Students react to the specific more out of habit or personal feelings or observation than out of the abstract ideas in the management literature.

To help a student to confront these gaps is not to say that there is any one best way to manage or that the student is wrong – merely to point out that one way or another, the gap between theory and application may need to be closed.

If management is, as I believe, a performing art, then it is both theory and performance that students need to be helped to learn. We would think it a strangely inadequate sort of music education if performers learned to analyze and discuss music and critique musical performances, but were able to play only at a very elementary level. In teaching management, we often do a much better job of theory (and credentialing students) than we do of developing practical skills.

I do not want to fall into the trap of saying that there is only one best way to teach. The teaching methods need to fit the course objectives, the curriculum, the students, the faculty, the school — all the many elements of the situation. Teachers are managers of their classrooms, and as such need to approach it very much in the way real-life managers approach their roles in work organizations. I believe that the full range of learning methods, including the experiential, may not be used because of a traditional emphasis on verbal learning. (Even if it looks like a manager and talks like a manager and thinks like a manager, it may not be able to manage.)

In teaching basic management graduate courses, I found particularly useful a couple of devices which seemed to help students focus on this theory-practice gap. (I also used the traditional reading, writing, lecturing, group process, etc. as part of the mix.)

One was the Application of Learning exercise (which I did not originate, but adapted to my purposes). Students are asked at the end of major classroom or individual segments to consider specifically what they have learned from the segment, how it might be (or has been) applied by them in real life, and what they see as possible strengths and weaknesses of the ideas in action. To make it more rigorous, students put this in writing and pass it in for review. (If students report that they have learned nothing useful, the question simply shifts to why, or why not, and what this might indicate.)

The other device is for the students to compile all of their written material in a Work Book as the course progresses. This includes material collected and commented upon as well as their own writing. Periodically, the teacher reviews these and provides feedback in some detail. At this point, there is not an over-all grade, but the feedback clearly implies a general performance level.

As in real life, these evaluations give students an option: they may at any later time during the course review and rewrite any of their material, in the light of the evaluation. They do not have to do this, but they do have the option. The earlier material is left in the Workbook, but the revision becomes the basis for the later reviews and the course evaluation. The traditional classroom test checks what you know and can write in a class period, and grades it. The Workbook method I used replaced midterm and final examinations. Students also received evaluations and comments on class participation during the course. At the end of the course, students received a letter course grade (as the academic system requires).

An interesting shift occurs with many students when they encounter a class situation more like the work experience and more oriented toward putting theory into action. Some students feel liberated and respond very positively. Some find the adjustment very difficult. Most of my students assess the courses (in anonymous written feedback both during the course and at the end) as involving both more work and more learning than usual.

I should add that this feedback process was a major source to me for adjusting and refining course materials and methods. With mature adult students, many with significant work experience, their input is particularly helpful – not necessarily in terms of group responses, but in useful individual suggestions as well. In-class discussions which pause to exchange reactions after course experiences can also be a very useful dialogue.

In teaching, as with managing, it is not a matter of discovering or inventing some unique technique. I suspect just about everything has been done somewhere. Nor is it a matter of picking up a standard practice: we need more flexibility, more willingness to depart from the classic classroom routine (as excellent teachers have always done).

I believe it is the process of managing the classroom, of shaping and reshaping it to fit situations which are always to some degree unique, of constantly learning in action, which can make teaching management such a challenge and (when things go well) such a joy.

Chapter Twenty-one

MANAGEMENT DEAN

IT IS ONE thing to be a teacher. It is quite a different thing to be a Dean. At JFK University, I was both a management professor and Dean of the School of Management – a wonderful combination of teaching and applying management in both roles in a small, supportive organization. It was the best management job I ever had.

The contrast with the University of California could not have been greater. To move the vast UC system a few inches often took years of patient effort and the cooperation of multitudes of people, known and unknown. To micro-manage the academic affairs of a small professional School of Management, I could work face-to-face with faculty, students and administrators and make changes in days or weeks – and often see the results soon after that.

JFKU had few resources, a relatively short history, and a not-too-secure future. It had high hopes, great visions, fragile finances, and a positive but regional reputation. Its strength was in the kind of people it attracted as faculty, students, and staff. They had to enjoy its opportunities rather than be discouraged by its limits.

The University kept its costs very low. It leased surplus public school buildings at a time when there were fewer school children. The school district got modest income and was able to keep and maintain the facilities for possible future needs. Part-time faculty mostly relied on their full-time work for basic income. Modest stipends and few benefits for teachers was acceptable because they were doing it as a professional service for a non-profit organization and for the students. It was extra money (and anyway, the teaching, not the money, was the main reward.) The physical plant had a sort of low-cost improvised charm which suited the informal style of the school.

The basic academic concept of the School of Management – bringing together the management of business, public, and non-profit organizations in a single school – was also innovative at the time. Many universities had separate graduate business schools (MBA) and public administration schools (MPA). Some had programs in the management of various specific types of organizations (schools, hospitals, welfare, local government, arts, etc.). What was uncommon seemed to me the most sensible: a school which took the management of organizations of all kinds as its focus.

In this approach, students could both specialize in a particular area of management and learn about areas common to all organizations. Business schools, the dominant and still-growing traditional type, tended to lump all kinds of management into the business area. The implication seemed to be that all organizations should be managed like businesses – if you could manage a business you could manage anything. To me, it makes more sense that all organizations have some management fundamentals in common and some unique aspects as well. No one type of organization should be the management model.

I enjoyed building a curriculum around this concept, teaching courses which reflected it, and helping students benefit from it. The founding dean told me later that the idea of a Management school originated when JFKU was too small to have separate schools of business, government, etc. If it was an economic choice, it was also a creative concept and had fortunate academic consequences. For one thing, alternative schools need to have distinctive academic niches. Merely to imitate and duplicate what is already available in larger and more traditional schools is futile and likely to fail.

Another factor which helped the School of Management was the interest and support of some business, government and non-profit organizations in the area. Their help was not the sort of corporate gifts and government grants which flow to prestigious research institutions. Many local organizations saw the need for advanced management education for some of their employees. It was important to them that employees who wanted to participate in management degree programs be able to do so close to home and work and on a convenient schedule. It provided a useful supplement to training and development programs for employees willing to make the added effort, and enabled them to continue their education. Employers were willing to pay all or part of the cost as long as grades and progress were satisfactory. It was a fringe benefit targeted to a specially motivated group.

The low tuition and practical teaching led many employers to encourage people to consider our offerings. Not all of the students had employer assistance – some were preparing to return to the labor force or to make a career change from some other field – but the employer assisted group was large enough to give a stable enrollment base of about 300 students.

No organization is without problems, including young and attractive ones like JFKU:

- Academic quality. It is one thing to outline innovative programs and another to see that they actually give what they promise. With part-time faculty and relatively open admissions, how do you monitor the quality of faculty and students?

  Faculty hiring was informal and did not involve tenure. We could reward excellence and deal with shortcomings very directly and individually. There were a variety of useful information sources – verified professional education and experience; review of course materials; one-to-one discussions, group faculty sessions on teaching, reviews of grade patterns, student evaluations (formal and informal), etc.. All these processes were useful for the Dean and for the small group of particularly experienced teachers who were the core faculty of the School.

  Quality meant not only professional and teaching qualifications in the usual sense, but a match with our particular kind of students and school. I learned that some people very capable in every other respect were simply not well suited to our needs. Fortunately, these often self-selected out when they figured this out for themselves. In interactive small-group teaching, one cannot help but be aware of student attitudes. One cannot use the protection of lectern and lecture to remain remote from the group, as is possible with traditional teaching.

  We had at the time a large pool of teaching applicants from which to select. Many excellent teachers who would not be available full-time would enjoy part-time teaching, particularly as the school could be flexible in schedules. Some faculty taught every quarter, sometimes more than one course; others taught only at intervals and repeated a particular course as needed.

Still, it is not always easy to approach a classroom with full vigor and enthusiasm after a full and perhaps hectic working day. This applies to both students and faculty. I usually found the classroom experience a tonic. Nevertheless, any tendency to "make allowances" and to expect less of part-time students or faculty threatens quality. It is necessary in non-traditional education to be alert to the difference between innovation and relaxed standards.

- Accreditation. There are two kinds of accreditation which apply to universities and to graduate programs like JFKU. One is the periodical review by a regional body, to determine whether the university meets quality standards set by the accrediting agency. The other is the accreditation of academic programs by national groups, each of which deal with a particular part of the university curriculum.

While institutions can and do exist which are not accredited (in the over-all university sense), it makes a powerful difference whether a university is accredited or not. Financial aid may not be available. Employers may refuse employee reimbursement. Degrees may be regarded as sub-standard. Students may go elsewhere.

Accreditation is a useful concept: self-governing quality control among higher education institutions. It has a long and useful history. It is sometimes difficult, however, to distinguish in the accrediting process between maintaining standards of quality (which may be met in diverse ways) and requiring standard operations (which may or may not relate directly to quality).

JFKU had been an accredited university before I arrived and it continued to be accredited during two reviews which happened while I was there. I found the process time-consuming but helpful, with one worrisome exception.

There tends to be an assumption in accreditation reviews that full-time faculty is the quality norm, that part-time faculty is a temporary aberration, and that schools should be moving toward primary use of full-time faculty.

This exerts a pressure on non-traditional universities which may in time eliminate a useful teaching model. It seems to me more a matter of insisting on a traditional way of operating than of maintaining quality. Any over-supply of full-time teachers may tend to increase the pressure on their behalf.

- Business School Accreditation. National organizations of business schools (as well as public administration school groups) develop recommended professional standards which must be met in order to be accredited in their academic field. Schools may participate as members of these organizations whether or not they seek accreditation, which is optional.

In larger and more traditional schools, the edicts of the business school establishment are powerful. Business schools and their faculties strive to meet the standards, and may use them as a shield ("We have to follow the national standards for accreditation.") Newer and smaller schools and their faculty see "full accreditation" as a prestigious goal. Instead of pursuing their own visions, they may tend to go by the handy accreditation checklist.

One might think that the power of a national professional group would help focus attention on promising new alternatives. This was true to some extent in the public administration area. In business schools (then in a boom phase of growth) I found much self-satisfaction but little interest in non-traditional alternatives.

When I went to the national meetings of business school groups in search of new ideas, I encountered a good deal of arrogance and snobbery, a lot of status-seeking, and little real interaction. I have had colleagues at such meetings turn away or ignore me entirely when they found I was from an unimportant little school. (I had often represented the University of California at national meetings of other groups; the contrast was enlightening.)

To balance the account, I must mention with gratitude a distinguished Harvard Business School professor, living in retirement in the Bay Area. He was the academic mentor I needed – open minded and perceptive – a volunteer consultant of a calibre I never could have afforded, who only thought of helping our school shape its curriculum. Similarly, the head of a large Middlewestern public administration program (a distinguished scholar, as well) took a warm personal interest in our school and encouraged us in what we were doing at JFK. Such exceptional help from such truly prestigious individuals was particularly appreciated.

The force of habit. Innovative and alternative schools are vulnerable to the grinding forces of habit and convention, which tend over time to wear away the distinctive features and make an innovative program more ordinary, more mainstream, more safe. As people come into the organization who were not part of the original vision or who do not fully accept it, conservative tendencies are likely to grow.

For example JFKU took some pride in its frugal, ad hoc facilities. (The founding myth of the university went back to its struggling start in a former mortuary building.) After twenty years of this, however, some people yearned for more comfort, more space, better offices, better image.

The administrative style at JFKU was also frugal and ad hoc, but as time went on some people wanted the place to run more like other schools, and to provide the more familiar structure of services and procedures.

JFKU took pride in its low tuition, its relatively open access, its diverse student body. The feeling was that students should be allowed to succeed or fail in the classroom, not in the admissions office, so long as they could meet minimum entrance standards. By the time JFKU was twenty years old, some said that if fees were higher the faculty and staff could be better paid and that if entrance was more restricted the school would have more prestige.

In time, fewer people could speak directly of the "old days" and the original vision and struggle of the school. More important, people coming in brought with them from elsewhere their ideas of what a school should be. Those who had been at more traditional or affluent schools tended to see them as the more desirable norm. Even those drawn to a distinctive school did not necessarily all have the same expectations.

In short, to maintain the vision and the energy of innovation becomes more difficult over time. Even success can be a problem. Is it innovative to keep on doing something which was new when it started but which has become increasingly common? Few universities had a focus on advanced degree evening programs for part-time working adult students. There turned out to be a tremendous need: mid-career professional education, life-long learning, career changes, workforce reentry. But after twenty years, other schools were catching on, some with much greater resources and marketing experience.

Do you stay with your original niche, even as the competition grows – or do you need to continue to experiment, to change focus, to keep on the cutting edge? Or some mix of both? What is the proper combination?

I suspect that at a place like JFKU, part of the answer lies in turnover. It is a rare person who can sustain indefinitely a commitment to continual innovation. Along with the satisfactions of such an organization come heavy demands. It may be better for many people as a short-term place rather than a long-term career. If people come, do what they came to do or are able to do, and move on, the organization may be able to renew and revise itself more or less indefinitely.

After five years as Dean at JFKU, I reached that point. I had done most of what I had joined JFKU to do, and felt the proportion of routine maintenance rising. The school needed new leadership to keep on reinventing its programs for changing times and changing needs. I continued teaching there for another five years, until I felt the need for some new challenge. (Perhaps to write a book?) It was better for the school and better for me that I move on.

PART FIVE

PUTTING IT TOGETHER

Snapshot (1990)

WHO IS THIS person that I see in mirrors and in photos – seventyish, balding, white-haired, tri-focaled, shorter and more unimpressive than ever? Who is this older guy? When did I turn into my father?

How can that be me? All those other self-images from all those decades past are still there in some curious overlay. Press some memory button and all kinds of internal selves respond.

By this time, I really am retired, but only in the sense of not being employed and not wanting to be. I still don't like some implications of the term. All it means to me is that I have a wider range of choices about what to do, since payment is no longer a factor. My general rule of thumb is to choose things that are satisfying and worthwhile. (Except, of course the increasing time spent on personal maintenance and repair, which is worthwhile but not always satisfying.)

Most satisfying is still marriage and family – or rather, families. Approaching fifty years together, Betty and I have become so deeply joined that one would be incomplete without the other. There are now three other families, too – independent, as we were independent, but still linked to us and to one another and to other families in loving network. Five grandchildren now – connecting us again to childhood and adolescence, and to our own and our children's.

This has been a very long generation. It feels like a time to get off the stage, to take only bit parts and background roles, to be more audience than actor, to watch the incredible energy of those in the young and middle years, and to marvel at the complex demands on that energy. It is a time to help, if you can.

For me, now feels so much less stressful than then – more choices and fewer demands. It is a satisfying decade, except – perhaps – for this nagging impulse to try to understand what happened and why.

When it comes to looking at the past, there is a lot of help these days. I've never seen such an outpouring of nostalgia. It seems to be the fiftieth anniversary of practically everything – from high school and college graduation on. In the performing arts, revivals are the big thing. Everything seems to be on film or tape, and sooner or later it shows up again – even the things you didn't particularly like the first time around.

As the end of the century approaches, it feels as if we want more to look back than ahead. After the fiftieth anniversary binge, it will soon be time to review the whole century (and, no doubt, to observe the thousand-year turning of the calendar as well).

Is all this mere fin-de-siecle trauma or trumped-up commercial use of times past? Partly, it is also a sort of procrastination, I suspect, a feeling that so much is bad that we don't want to think about it. If you feel powerless to shape the future, why think about it? The past is safer – you know how things turned out then.

I understand now why it can be easy in older years to feel more conservative, more fearful, more anxious, more resistant to changes. You have lived long enough to learn of more bad things that can happen. You sense how many things could go wrong and how little you can do about them.

Somehow the crises of the past remain sharp and clear ("Where were you when Kennedy was shot?" – everybody in my generation has a ready answer.) The good times, the long stretches of happiness, even the great good-luck fortunate happenings – all of these seem to merge into a general background blur.

Perhaps a managerial attitude can provide an antidote to these negative tendencies. Managers learn from the past, but only to improve their ability to cope with and to shape the future. When managers look back, it is more likely to be a part of the process of looking ahead. Rather than feeling depressed at their accumulated knowledge of problems past, managers tend to feel optimistic that somehow with this increased knowledge they are more likely next time to get it right.

That makes sense to me. I still believe that the future can be better than the past and the present – if we can manage to make more use of what we know.

Chapter Twenty-two

MAKING MANAGEMENT SENSE

HAVING SAID IN so many ways that there is no one best way, it would be inappropriate to conclude with some summary of management principles. The subject needs to be left open.

I hope that the material – both the specific incidents and the career-long sequence of events – has helped you get inside the head of a manager and learn more about management. Along the way, I have expressed some of my own feelings and conclusions, but again I want to emphasize that what you learn from reading them is mainly up to you. What you learn may be very different from what I experienced. You need to apply it to yourself and to your situation and to what you are trying to do.

However, this process may be helped by stating some more general thoughts – ideas which developed out of my experiences and have helped me make sense of management.

- Managers develop a special kind of reality – a functional picture of the organization and its environment. The process of becoming a manager – or of understanding what managers do and why they do it – involves developing some such simplified version of reality. Like most specialists, managers learn to ignore a great many things which do not seem to them useful of necessary for their purposes.

  For example, most people in a large organization are not seen by a manager as real individuals. There are too many of them to know personally or even to see face-to-face, so they become something else – positions, duties statements, numbers, employees, personnel, human resources, etc. – according to management's needs to know. Interest in their motivations and feelings may be limited to a few simple managerial assumptions.

Managers do much of their work rather quickly by relying uncritically on habits and generalizations (so long as they seem to work reasonably well). Consciously or not, they do this to prevent information overload and decision stalemate. Managers simplify reality in order to make sense out of a reality which would otherwise be overwhelmingly complex.

Even so, an important part of management skill is in making satisfactory judgments on the basis of limited and inadequate information. The art of getting it together is the art of making sense out of the things you know – or think you know – and making good guesses about the rest.

The pictures in a manager's head make it possible to take appropriate action, provided they are updated often enough. Things always are changing. No two situations are alike. The gap between the "reality" picture and the real world must not become too large.

It helps to think of managers as working in this way, rather than as all-knowing, all-wise and all-powerful. Managers are just regular people who – like doctors, lawyers, ministers, politicians, teachers, and other specialists – have developed some extraordinary work skills (often at the expense of other capabilities).

- Managers tend to identify themselves with the organization. Managers (and potential managers) are more likely, I believe to mean both themselves and the organization in which they work when they say "we." Other specialists are likely to say "we" when they mean themselves and their fellow specialists, whether they are in the same organization or not.

This attachment to the organization helps give meaning and value to the management role. The over-all survival and welfare of the organization provides the energizing purpose as well as the sense of status and prestige. Others often share in this perception: that managers actually seem larger and more imposing in the context of their offices and organizations than elsewhere.

As managers have become more specialized (as I believe they have), this identification may go through a curious reversal: what is good for the manager becomes what the manager sees as good for the organization. There is still a close identification, but it is the welfare of the manager which energizes the organization. If this happens, the "we" really does become the manager or the executive group, not the whole organization.

Managers also try very hard to get as many other people as possible to identify with the organization and its management. Because of the many centrifugal forces which work against unity, particularly in large organizations, this may be a necessary and appropriate leadership task. On the other hand, one needs to watch carefully what is done as well as what is said in order to get the real message.

- Management can be a very portable skill, but there are limits and risks. As I moved among some very different organizations, I found (as I expected) that there was a large amount of carry-over of management learning and skills, but with each transition it needed to be reinterpreted and adapted. There are also some limits, both organizational and personal. Some organizations just do not accept the idea of general management. Either they do not see management as a function at all – as, until recently, many colleges, universities, and churches did not – or they think themselves so unique as to make managerial experience elsewhere inapplicable – as in many hospitals, schools and charities.

There are also limits for the manager. At one time, I was confident (for example) that I could in general do my managerial thing in almost any type of organization. I found later that I needed to have a real and continuing interest in the organization mission. A further limitation developed eventually: I also needed to be sympathetic with the values and processes by which the organization works. I need to care about both the ends and the means in order to make the needed commitment as a manager.

- Managers need to prefer to get things done indirectly, not directly. This seems at odds with the picture of managers as power-hungry bosses who try to run everything and everybody. There are, of course, such managers, but the more typical manager does not want to do everything personally. In larger organizations, the manager may well not even want personally to see that everything is done – better to leave that, too, to others.

In this sense, a potential manager may seem a bit lazier than others – getting some things done through persuading others to do it, if possible. This may include some upward management: potential managers are more likely to hone their skills by passing problems and ideas to their bosses, rather than just receiving work assignments.

When it is promotion time, this may create a problem. The unspoken assumption in the workplace is often that promotion will be (or at least should be) a reward for superior work performance. The person who does the best work should be promoted. Fair enough, at first.

When the move is to supervisor or manager, however, the equation may change. Demonstrated work skills are still important, but the person selected also needs to be able to get work done with and through others. The dedicated and able employee may be thought more useful to the organization in the "hands on" job, or be considered likely to have difficulty in leaving direct work to others less skilled. Unfortunately, many organizations give out very mixed messages about this. It is best to review not only the promotion policies but the actual practices as well, for guidance.

A corollary is that if you are interested in management you should exercise your curiosity and pay attention to a lot of things which are not strictly necessary to do your day-to-day job. This should include studying your bosses and others in positions important to your present or future work.

- Circumstances and luck play a large part in determining a management career. It is natural for people with a managerial inclination to feel some confidence that they can make things happen through and with other people – including becoming a manager and making major career moves. When it happens, advancement is likely to seem in retrospect a personal accomplishment

It is healthy to recall as well the other circumstances which also shape events. Rapid growth of an organization, for example, may open opportunities – if not one promotion, then another. (Down-sizing has, of course, the opposite effect; there may be few if any advancements, even for the highly qualified.)

Sometimes it is a matter of a certain fit. For example, I could take written and oral tests very well. The State government relied on such tests. On that basis alone, some opportunities were more available to me. The most I did was to choose an organization in which that ability was particularly useful.

It is also useful to see how little lasting impact a manager usually has on an organization. The key word here is "lasting." Managers can and do have major impacts on organizations. Organizations are, however, often very resilient and tend to persist in their own character as managers come and go. When they do change, there are so many factors and so many people involved that in the long run the changes seem impersonal. Managers leave few monuments. Ten years, or even five years later, it is often difficult to put your finger on anything you, a former manager, left as a personal legacy. (Construction projects can be a satisfying exception to the general rule.)

A reasonable amount of humility helps managers keep their roles and their accomplishments in perspective. Organizations both elevate and frustrate their leaders. Managers are not royalty among commoners. They usually lead more by consensus than command. In truth, they need to be (as much as anything else) lucky.

Chapter Twenty-three

MANAGER IN ACTION

If managers do not simply learn principles and techniques and apply them (and I am convinced that they do not and should not), then what is it that managers really do or should do? Without resorting to oversimplification, can we somehow put it all together in action?

Managers specialize in getting things done in work organizations, primarily with and through other people, particularly in organizations which are too large to operate as a face-to-face group and with a special responsibility for accomplishing the over-all goals of the organization. Their basic job is to lead the organization. Managers do a lot of other things – some of which are not necessarily management – but that is their basic role. Managers are not wiser or better or more important than other people because of what they do. They have an interesting and complex and vital role to play which affects everyone else in the organization. They have skills which can be learned and practiced and improved.

Now, let's go back to the beginning. The most important thing to learn as a manager is how to keep on learning. I hope you will go back over some of the experiences in this book and analyze them – learn from them, pick out things you could put into action (or consider why some things might not work for you), and decide when and how to try out those which seem of most immediate use in your situation.

Then I hope you will start thinking back over your own experiences and ideas in much the same way, seeing what you can learn from them and how you might keep on learning from them. Consider your present situation and what you are trying to do. How might you try some new ways of getting things done and of relating to others?

Personal experience is probably your best teacher (if you go back and review it honestly and critically), but your work life is too short to learn only by personal trial and error. Use the experiences of others, too. Seek out management literature and keep up with current developments. Look for opportunities to study management as a student (or teacher).

Remember that your goal is not merely to know about or to think about various aspects of management, but to put them into action in whatever ways are appropriate to your situation. The more you practice, the more you are likely to learn to use more of your personal potential as a manager. If you accept that management is primarily a performing art, it makes sense that learning it should be a life-long process of continuing experiment, growth and change.

You may want to start with self-management in your work life. Consider, for example, (1) things which you are required to do in your work (and how you might do them better), (2) things you want to do in your work (and how you might accomplish more within the limits of your situation), (3) your relationships with others, and how they might become more satisfactory and effective in your work life. Consider both immediate needs and long-term possibilities.

Next to your own ability to manage yourself, you will probably find that it is your relationships which are the most important. In organizations you are always dependent to some extent on others, and vice versa. Relationships can both help and hurt your activities. You need to understand yourself, and as much as possible you need also to understand what are trying to do. There is no reason you cannot try to make relationships work better for all concerned, rather than accepting them as if they are somehow too mysterious or too firmly established to change. (We are not talking about psychological probing here, but merely a functional sensitivity to what tends to work well (or not) in your work situation.

Many of the things you learn will probably be specific to your work life. In general, however, we are probably talking about trust, communication, mutual support, group teamwork, commitment, and the like. It may be better to start with what others need from you, and how you can respond better in what you do. It is natural to think of your own needs – we tend to think of ourselves as the center of any organization to which we belong. It is sensible, however, to realize that others are more likely to respond if they feel you have empathy for them and are not merely looking for your own advantage.

We have often referred to "what you are trying to do" at work. Where does this come from? Certainly not from the usual job descriptions, which try to spell out how your tasks and activities are different from those of others. They tend to establish territories, but shed little light on the dynamics of relationships and the realities of goals and values. Your sense of "what you are trying to do" will be influenced to some extent by everyone and everything with which you are in contact. As you put it together, some parts will be logical and clear and structured. Some will be vague hunches and guesses and feelings. As you learn from experience, both aspects will evolve. Keep flexible and open to change. Remember also that you should be as concerned with how you respond to others as to what you need from others. Most of your work is probably initiated by somebody else.

My own experience is that as you muddle around and work on things bit by bit and are sensitive both to logic and to feelings, the sense of "what you are trying to do" comes together in action. You find yourself knowing as a result of doing (and sometimes the answers are surprising).

You don't have to understand exactly how this works (I think nobody does). Just keep open and let it happen and hope for the best. Expect improvement with practice. Managers have to be optimistic and full of positive energy about the future. As in sports, there's always another season – maybe next time, maybe next year.

I believe that how you feel about yourself and your work organization is crucial. I can work effectively in an organization if I believe in its basic purposes and values and if I feel good about my place in it. Unless I have these feelings, I tend over time to lose energy and confidence and commitment. (Of course, there are also some negative motivators; if I have no ready alternative, I can work in a bad situation as long as I have to – but that sort of negative pressure eventually takes a personal toll.)

If you feel good about yourself in your work life, if you can be optimistic (but realistic) about what you are doing and what you can do, I believe your chances of success are somehow much greater. If you can visualize your success, it may help it in some way to become real. (Unfortunately, I think the same thing tends to apply to negative feelings. One needs to be aware of the inevitable down-sides of relationships and organizations without being depressed by them.)

A way to look at your work life and particularly at the mix of positive and negative factors may be to consider it as a combination of situations, each composed of many elements. Some situations can be changed easily, others are fixed (at least for the present), and others might change or be changed depending on further developments.

It would be rare to find all the elements of a situation compatible with one another, or to find all your situations neatly fitting together. As you consider what you are trying to do, some aspects will be positive and some negative and some neutral and some uncertain in their impact. The first step is to believe in the possibility – even the likelihood – of developing a creative solution which fits with the whole situation (by creative, I mean a new and more effective way of solving a problem or achieving a purpose.)

Most people think they have very few choices, because they look only at the obvious ones. Many people think it is a question of power: you have to have power over others to make them do what you want done (overlooking that such power is not only untypical but tends when it does occur to generate opposing powers). Others see compromise as the only possible solution – give a little here, take a little there, bargain it out to gain as much of what you want as you can get. The assumption here is that what I win you lose, and vice versa.

Sometimes these approaches are needed, but I believe that what Mary P. Follette called "creative integration" is often the best way and should usually be the preferred way. The best way (she said) of getting something done in complex situations is often to find a solution which works within the limits of the situation and meets the real needs of those involved.

As she points out, one cannot simply ask people what they want. One has to use real empathy and careful analysis of behavior to figure out, all things considered, what (beneath the surface chatter) are probably the real motivations.

Approached in this way, with a commitment to creating win-win solutions and programs, it is surprising how often some new and successful approach can be found which goes a long way toward meeting everyone's needs. Much of this book illustrates how this has worked in my own experiences.

It is not sure-fire. It is not simple. It is not revolutionary, except perhaps in the quiet way in which situations can seem to change from stalemate and conflict to progress and agreement. Things tend to go better with this approach. At the same time, one must forego the doubtful pleasures of flaunting power and authority and of demanding personal credit if it is to succeed. You can feel good about yourself and how you deal with people and what you are accomplishing, but do not demand or expect general acclaim. When it works the best, your role is likely to be at least low-profile and perhaps invisible.

In practice, one of the hardest things is to get out of the habit of either-or thinking and into a both-and approach. It is easy to see managers as dealing with a series of conflicting opposites: boss-subordinate, management-labor, centralized-decentralized, trusting-defensive, powerful-weak, allies enemies, short-term/long-term, passive-aggressive, win-lose, we-they, top-bottom, this-that — — whatever, the list can be endless. This way of thinking encourages the idea that one has to win and the other to lose. Often the best answer for all concerned is neither to win nor to lose but to develop something in between, something new which fits a particular situation and moves things along in a way which meets everybody's needs as much as is possible — including of course your personal needs.

This search for creative integration, for win-win solutions, for both-and approaches, is not a soft or idealistic way to manage. Although it lacks the macho excitement of the traditional "tough boss" manager or "power-driven" politician, it requires some tough qualities: self-confidence, commitment, patience, empathy, intellect, trust, vision, creativity, realism, and even a certain amount of modesty.

I believe that this situational approach offers managers a difficult and challenging role, but also offers the possibility of a work environment in which people (including managers) can use more of their talents, develop more positive relationships, and accomplish more. Ultimately, I guess I would say, "Try it, even if in a very small way. See what happens. It might work. You might like it. At the least, you could probably learn something about management from the experience."

AFTERTHOUGHT (1995)

THERE IS MORE to life than work – and more to work than management.

Management makes sense in relation to work organizations. That's what it is about: a particular kind of life at work. It can be a very absorbing and demanding work. In a sense, it is never done and surely never done well enough. A manager can easily be drawn in so deeply that work life and work identity become nearly all-consuming.

For me, the most useful secret of management is that in the long run you need a good life in order to be a good manager. Some people keep work life at bay and in its place by thinking of it as a limited means to a more important end – hours paid in exchange for money to finance whatever really matters to them in their personal lives. Others delay most of life until some hoped-for better time.

I realize that for a great many people there do not seem to be many choices. Their situations have much tighter limits than mine have ever had. I believe, though, that over time most people have some choices, however small, and it is generally better to use whatever choices you have.

My suggestion is that, to the extent you can, you look neither to your work nor to your personal life for your self-esteem and satisfactions. Look to both. Use whatever choices you have to integrate them. Be a whole person with a whole life, and decide what that means to you.

If you are a manager (or a prospective manager), don't always put the job first. Don't always put it last, either. Do what you have to do. Do what satisfies you. Do what helps you live the life you want. But relate it to the rest of your life.

Don't leave your personal life for whatever time and energy (if any) is left from work. Sometimes one will dominate your attention and sometimes the other will – both have their seasons. But no matter what the current balance, plan both as a whole. Some of the most important things in life mean nothing at work but give life its meaning. Some of the most important things at work help give life its meaning, too. They need to interact.

Try to be as much as possible the same person at work and in the rest of your life. The management role – and all your other roles – need to be performed in a way which is not only within your range but which feels comfortable to your inner self.

Management may ultimately be nothing more than a way of making sense of organizations and of your work life. Learning to do that is a lifelong task – but that task should also be part of a larger quest, one which goes far beyond management.

But that, of course, is another story.

www.ingramcontent.com/pod-product-compliance
Lightning Source LLC
LaVergne TN
LVHW091643100826
845152LV00007B/151/J

* 9 7 8 1 9 3 6 9 4 0 0 6 6 *